50 Ways to Engage Students with Google Apps

50 Ways to ENGAGE STUDENTS with Google Apps

Alice **KEELER**

Heather **LYON**

50 Ways to Engage Students with Google Apps
© 2024 Alice Keeler and Heather Lyon

All rights reserved. No part of this publication may be reproduced in any form or by any electronic or mechanical means, including information storage and retrieval systems, without permission in writing by the publisher, except by a reviewer who may quote brief passages in a review. For information regarding permission, contact the publisher at books@daveburgessconsulting.com.

> This book is available at special discounts when purchased in quantity for educational purposes or for use as premiums, promotions, or fundraisers. For inquiries and details, contact the publisher at books@daveburgessconsulting.com.

Published by Dave Burgess Consulting, Inc.
San Diego, CA
DaveBurgessConsulting.com

Library of Congress Control Number: 2023950055
Paperback ISBN: 978-1-956306-73-6
Ebook ISBN: 978-1-956306-74-3

Cover and Interior design by Liz Schreiter
Edited and produced by Reading List Editorial
ReadingListEditorial.com

Contents

Introduction: Engaging Students with Google Tools 1
    Defining Student Engagement 2
    Instructional Design and Engaging Learners 10
    Using This Book 13

50 Ways to Engage Students with Google Apps 16
    1. Breaking Patterns 16
    2. Interacting with Readers 18
    3. Using Active Learning 20
    4. Offering Choices 22
    5. Scratching the Mystery 24
    6. Reducing Participation Anxiety 25
    7. Sorting for Critical Thinking 26
    8. Jumping to Feedback 27
    9. Encouraging Group Discussion 29
    10. Choosing from Categories 30
    11. Constraining Options 32
    12. Checking for Fluency 34
    13. Fostering a Low Risk of Failure 35
    14. Creating Clubs 37
    15. Choosing the Questions 38
    16. Incorporating Personal Interests 39
    17. Recording Text Feedback 41
    18. Focusing on the Product 42
    19. Replacing Assignments 43
    20. Targeting for All, Most, Some 44
    21. Checking In and Out 46
    22. Tracking Growth 48
    23. Noticing and Wondering 50
    24. Hyperlinking Google Slides 52
    25. Earning Badges 54
    26. Checking for Feedback 56
    28. Hosting Virtual Parent Meetings 59
    29. Forming Groups 61
    30. Personalizing with Names 64
    31. Rethinking Learning Loss 66
    32. Rebranding with Gamification 68
    33. Creating with Pixel Art 70

34. Celebrating Success through Calls Home 71
35. Building Small Wins 73
36. Aiming for Mastery 74
37. Assessing the Standards 76
38. Rethinking Grading 77
39. Integrating Peer Feedback 79
40. Sharing in the Stream 80
41. Tapping into Student Expertise 82
42. Showing Growth with Student Portfolios 83
43. Embarking on Quest Chains 85
44. Choosing Adventure 87
46. Using Single-Point Rubrics 90
47. The Value of a Field Trip 91
48. Designing Collaborative Websites 93
49. Coding 94
50. Collaborating via Email 96

Conclusion 98
About the Authors 99
More from Dave Burgess Consulting, Inc. 103

Introduction:
Engaging Students with Google Tools

Google tools do not create student engagement. We would like to say this again: GOOGLE TOOLS DO NOT CREATE ENGAGEMENT. Tools do not teach. For students to learn—let alone be engaged in what they're learning—highly qualified teachers must carefully consider how they will use a variety of tools to apply pedagogical strategies.

Creating student engagement with Google tools means using them in innovative, unique ways. Google Slides is designed as a presentation tool, however in the twenty-first century students do not need teachers to present or "talk at" them in order to learn information. No student will be harmed because they do not know any particular fact. Google search is literally at our fingertips all of the time. Instead of using Google Slides as a presentation tool, we use it as a collaboration tool—for *students* to share their ideas and thinking about how they will approach a problem or apply a solution.

Google Sites is a website creation tool. Are Google Sites inherently fun and engaging? Definitely not. Alice uses Google Sites to post her syllabus and classroom expectations. Students are not any more excited about those things in class than if she had just handed them out on paper.

No one loves a spreadsheet more than Alice Keeler. "The answer is always a spreadsheet" is one of her mottoes. However, Alice frequently encounters someone who does not feel the same passion for spreadsheets as she does. For some, a spreadsheet is something scary. To win someone over to Google Sheets, Alice shows them how spreadsheets are fun and creative.

Using Google Classroom as a box to assign PDFs will not lead to student engagement. Google Classroom allows for unique ways to recognize students as individuals, which can increase engagement in a class.

Google Forms allows us to quickly see where students are struggling. Data by itself does not make a class more engaging, but seeing student responses easily allows for more efficient analysis and feedback—which does lead to more engagement.

With tongue firmly in cheek, Alice says, "Do not use Google Docs." Of course, she uses Google Docs, but other tools can be used more creatively and lead to an increase in student engagement.

DEFINING STUDENT ENGAGEMENT

Student engagement . . . Everyone says it, but what does that mean? The phrase is thrown around a lot when people really mean *compliance*. Tech companies promise to "engage students" and "measure student engagement" when they really are only recording the number of minutes online. "Students engaged with the activity for fifty minutes." No—students *interacted* with the assignment for fifty minutes. Some or all of those students, however, may have been bored out of their minds. In other words, despite the ubiquitous use of the word engagement, there is little to no agreement on what that word means. Without that consistency, it's very easy for one person to say a lesson is engaging while another person might view that same lesson as disengaging.

> Student engagement is not measured by the number of minutes completed nor the weight of how much was completed.

It was this lack of understanding and consistency around the definition of engagement that got Heather searching for a definition. Unfortunately, despite the fact that there are dozens, if not hundreds, of books written and marketed to educators about engagement, Heather couldn't find a book that really helped her define the term, though there were folks who helped shape her thinking. For example, Phillip Schlechty's work on engagement was a good starting point, as was Mihaly Csikszentmihalyi's book *Flow*. By combining bits and pieces of what others had shared with her own experiences in the classroom, Heather developed two critical pieces to pinpoint what engagement is and, just as importantly, is not.

The first aha she had was that engagement doesn't express itself in only one way. In other words, it's not an on/off switch—it's a dial. This means that there is an Engagement Continuum (see figure 1), with four different levels ranging from disengaged to engaged (see figure 2).

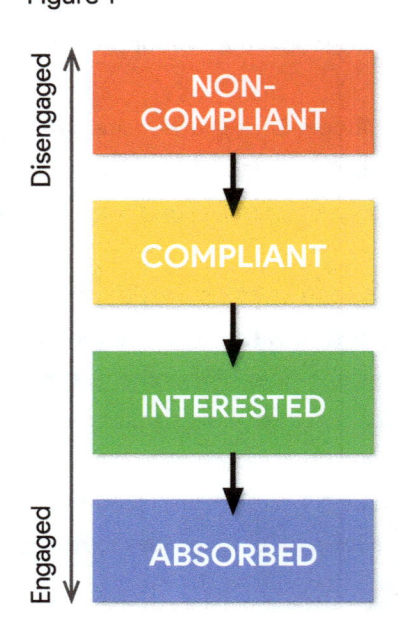

Figure 1

Disengaged ↑
NON-COMPLIANT
↓
COMPLIANT
↓
INTERESTED
↓
ABSORBED
Engaged ↓

Figure 2

THE FOUR LEVELS OF ENGAGEMENT
FROM *ENGAGEMENT IS NOT A UNICORN (IT'S A NARWHAL)*
BY HEATHER LYON

1. NON-COMPLIANT
Actively or passively refusing to do what was expected; insubordinate.

2. COMPLIANT
Doing the minimum of what was expected but only because of consequences (positive or negative).

3. INTERESTED
Going beyond the minimum expectations because the task is stimulating and has temporary value. Generally speaking, the task is enjoyable but not something that would be done unless it was required and there was a consequence for (not) doing it.

4. ABSORBED
Getting so involved in a challenging task that the person doing it intrinsically wants to continue even if they don't have to.

On the cover and throughout this book, you'll notice the image of a narwhal, and we'd like to take a moment to clarify its relevance to engagement. In her book *Engagement Is Not a Unicorn (It's a Narwhal),* Heather draws a comparison between mythical unicorns and real narwhals. While unicorns are purely fantastical, they are widely recognized. On the other hand, narwhals are real, even though many people don't recognize this fact.

Engagement can face a similar (mis)perception. Some view it as a mythical unicorn—an unreal concept. They imagine it to be out of reach, like the idea of students applauding the teacher at the end of a lesson, or as a ridiculously low bar, like a requirement that all students compliantly submit their homework on time. However, true engagement is more akin to students metaphorically applauding themselves and pursuing learning for its intrinsic value rather than merely chasing grades. This concept is not mythical. But like narwhals, it may not be as easy to find as we'd hope. Therefore, narwhals serve as a symbol, encouraging us to consider engagement beyond unrealistic myths and place it in a more realistic perspective.

It's only when people are interested or absorbed that they are really engaged. Though Heather was happy to have developed the Engagement Continuum, this linear representation did not help her understand why someone might be at any specific level or how to help them make a shift to a higher level of engagement. As both an educator and a parent, she wanted to be able to support others who might be at a lower level of engagement to shift to a higher level. If there was a way to do that, imagine the possibilities!

Good news: There is! She realized that there are important variables that cause people to shift engagement levels.

1. **How Do I Feel:** How a person feels about what they have to do has a major impact on whether or not they'll be engaged in it. If they like the task they're doing, they'll be engaged; if they don't like the task, they'll be disengaged.
2. **What Will I Get:** The consequences of doing a task are important. The term *consequence* is used in a neutral way here; it can be either positive (like money, candy, or another reward) or negative (like a fine, loss of privileges, or another punitive outcome). Consequences can be tricky—so more to come on them later.

3. **Who Says:** It can be very difficult for someone to engage in a task if the relationship with the person assigning it is negative. The opposite is true too: It can be easier for someone to engage in a task if the relationship with the person assigning it is positive. This certainly doesn't mean that a positive relationship always leads to engagement and vice versa, but it does mean that relationships between who assigns the task and who does that task impact engagement.

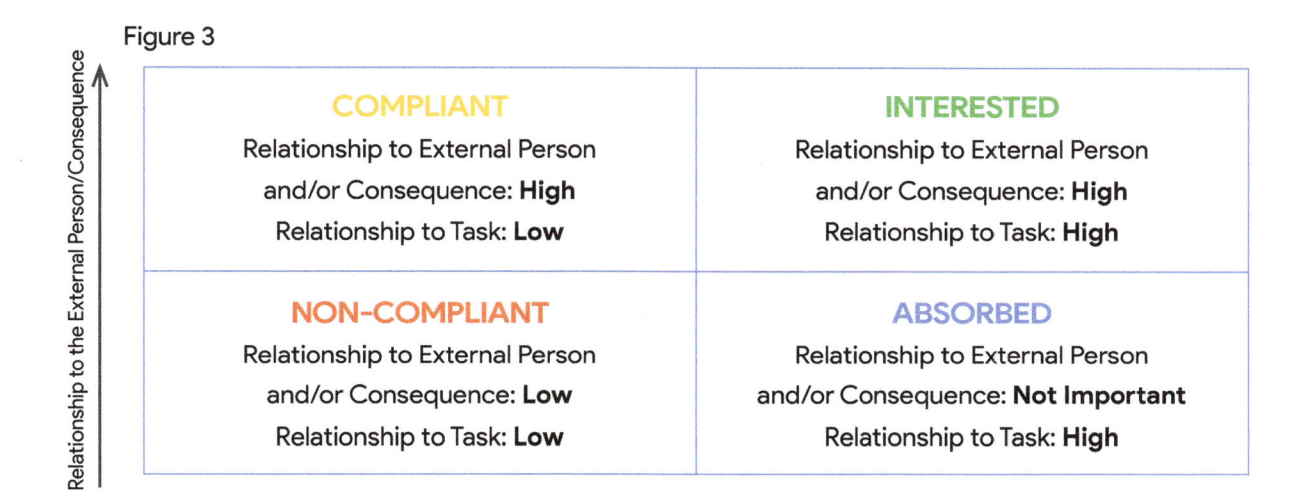

Figure 3

COMPLIANT Relationship to External Person and/or Consequence: **High** Relationship to Task: **Low**	**INTERESTED** Relationship to External Person and/or Consequence: **High** Relationship to Task: **High**
NON-COMPLIANT Relationship to External Person and/or Consequence: **Low** Relationship to Task: **Low**	**ABSORBED** Relationship to External Person and/or Consequence: **Not Important** Relationship to Task: **High**

Y-axis: Relationship to the External Person/Consequence
X-axis: Relationship to Task

All three of these factors led to the creation of the Engagement Matrix (see figure 3). Quite simply, the Engagement Matrix takes the four levels of engagement on the Engagement Continuum and bends them pole to pole. The relationship to the task is the horizontal axis, and the relationship to the extrinsic factors (i.e., the person assigning the task and/or the consequences for doing the task) are on the vertical axis.

This means that a non-compliant person has (a) a low relationship to the task (they don't like it), (b) a low relationship with the person assigning the task (they don't like them), and (c) a low relationship with the consequences for doing the task or not (they don't like the reward and don't care about the punishment). That can often sound like "I don't care about this, I don't care about you, and I don't care about what happens to me if I do or don't do this!"

On the other hand, a compliant person cares about the person assigning the task and/or the consequences for doing the task. Even so—and this is important—a compliant person does not want to do the task any more than a non-compliant person does. This is why these quadrants are on the left of the Engagement Matrix. The difference between a compliant person and a non-compliant person is that a compliant person is motivated extrinsically whereas a non-compliant person is not. Both, however, are disengaged.

> **It's obvious that people who are non-compliant are disengaged, however, what's less obvious is that compliant people are also disengaged.**

Interested people are engaged because they enjoy doing the task. However, interested people—like compliant people—are extrinsically motivated. Like compliant people, interested people respond well to the person assigning the task and/or the consequence for doing the task. Here the difference is that compliant people do not like what they're doing, but interested people do.

Finally, absorbed people, like interested people, enjoy the task they are doing. Unlike interest, which is extrinsically motivated, absorption is intrinsically motivated. Absorbed people do not need to have a strong relationship with the person assigning the task or place a high value on the consequence for doing the task since it is likely that absorbed people have either elected to do the task or wanted to do it anyway.

While Heather really liked the simplicity of the Engagement Continuum and the Engagement Matrix, there is a risk of oversimplification. With that in mind, there are a few very important points to consider here:

Remember Goldilocks. The first question people should ask when they recognize that someone is being non-compliant is whether or not the task the person is supposed to do is appropriately challenging for the person doing it. If not, the person will opt out. This could be because the task is too easy (if our task is to practice tying shoelaces one hundred times, we're going to opt out because we don't need to practice something we can do blindfolded). It could also be because the task is too hard (if our task is to perform brain surgery, we're going to opt out because we don't have the prerequisite skills). Even so, let's not forget that Goldilocks wanted the porridge the whole time—though you might call her non-compliant when she didn't finish Papa Bear or Mama Bear's porridge, she was hungry and did eat all of Baby Bear's porridge.

Not everyone is motivated identically. What motivates me is not going to work for everyone. This means that the better you know me, the more likely you will be to know what consequences will help improve my engagement.

Engagement can manifest in many ways. The reason behind someone's compliance, for example, may be their relationship with the person assigning the task—think, "I wouldn't do this for anyone else, but Grandma Elsie, I'll mow the lawn for you." Another person may be compliant with the same task not because they care about the relationship with the person assigning the task but because they care about the consequence for doing the task—think, "Mrs. Elsie Smith, I'll mow your lawn for $25." (See figure 4 for three different manifestations of each level of engagement.)

Figure 4

Manifestations of Engagement by Engagement Level	
Compliant	**Interested**
First Timer	Willing Participant
People Pleaser	Professional
Rule Follower	Strategist
Non-compliant	**Absorbed**
Rebel	Novice
Normalizer	Enthusiast
Activist	Addict

Heather Lyon, *The BIG Book of Engagement Strategies* (Alexandria, VA: Edumatch, 2021), 9.

Compliance is disengagement. It cannot be said enough: Since neither compliant people nor non-compliant people want to do what they're doing, both compliant and non-compliant people are disengaged. Compliance is simply when a disengaged person is extrinsically motivated to do the task. However, if someone has previously been non-compliant, compliance is a sign of growth and can be temporarily worthy of celebration as a step on the road to engagement.

Compliance with behaviors is not engagement with learning. In far too many classrooms, as long as students are compliant with the behavioral expectations ("Stay in your seat," "Do not shout out," etc.), they can be allowed to be non-compliant with learning expectations ("Read silently," "Work with a partner," etc.). Why? Students who are quiet and do not disrupt the learning of others can fall through the learning cracks because they do not draw negative attention to themselves. Therefore, many students learn very quickly that as long as they are quiet in class, the teacher will leave them alone regarding learning.

Change the task. Since only people who are interested or absorbed are engaged, in order to create engagement, people must have a high relationship with the task they are doing. Compliant people then must move rightward on the Engagement Matrix to become engaged. The way to do that is by changing the task. Certainly, there are some tasks that cannot be changed because they are required, like paying taxes. These are tasks that very few people will ever be interested in, let alone absorbed in. The academic goal of the work in schools is for students to achieve the standards. While we have little to no control over the standards, we have a great deal of control over what students can do to demonstrate their achievement of the standards. While changing the task might seem a little self-evident at first, classrooms often default to the tried and true, the known and familiar. Essays, end-of-chapter questions, worksheets, and the like are common compliance pitfalls. Teachers accept that though they are boring, these products get the job done. But the goal of engagement is more than getting the job done—it's getting students to enjoy the job.

And who doesn't want to enjoy their work?

Offer voice and choice. Voice and choice are similar in that both allow input, but voice means that the person doing the task creates the option(s) and choice means they select from the available options. It might happen that you are given both voice and choice. For example, it's your birthday and I ask you, "Where do you want to go for dinner?" That is *voice*. You can say the name of any restaurant. Once we get to that restaurant, you have to order off of the menu. That's *choice*. You need to select your choice based on the options provided. How can choice and voice happen in classrooms every day for every student? Choice can mean designing a menu of different tasks that will achieve the required learning. This means focusing on what the learning is supposed to be (the standards and the skills) and then designing at least two options that will achieve the learning. The students then have the all-important-to-engagement choice of what they will do in order to demonstrate their learning. Voice is even easier. The last choice of the options can always be "Propose an option that isn't listed that would meet the outcome." Certainly, if you have students who cannot yet read, there is work that needs to be done to help students understand this model, but even then it is possible.

Interest is temporary. Unlike compliant people, interested people enjoy the task they are doing. However, like compliance, interest requires extrinsic motivation. When/if that motivation goes away, so does engagement. Interested people will stop doing interesting work when given the chance to stop. For example, when the bell rings, how do the students react? Interested students pack up and leave *even if they were enjoying the work they were doing before the bell rang*. Is the project that they have been working on for weeks now over? Interested people will move on to the next assignment—they will not continue learning more about the project even if there is much more that could be learned. Interested people will do their homework, classwork, etc., but if you allow them to stop doing it, they will stop.

No one can be absorbed in everything. We have yet to find someone who isn't absorbed in something. Babies are absorbed in learning to do new things, children are often absorbed in their extracurricular activities, and adults are absorbed in hobbies (often, the things we pay to do). Even though absorption is the highest level of engagement, this is not the place to aim for every student, every day, in every classroom. Human beings are not wired to feel a constant high level of engagement in everything, and no two people find exactly the same things to be identically engaging or disengaging. Therefore, if you're aiming for absorption for all students every day, you're going to miss the mark. The aim should be to create *interest* for every student, in every classroom, every day.

Absorption needs both an intrinsic reward and an external challenge. Remember, to be absorbed means that you are willing to do the task beyond the point that you are able to stop; it is not limited to a time frame. Also, tasks that are absorbing require persistence, because we cannot achieve the highest levels of success the first time we attempt them. If we did, the task would be so easy that we would lose interest. Tasks that are absorbing require us to be gritty, for two reasons. First, we will need to devote a great deal of time and effort before we achieve the end goal, and, second, we will experience failure along the way, so we need to be resilient.

The bottom line when it comes to engagement is that it's really a pretty simple formula:

Enjoyment of the Task + Reward for the Task = Engagement

That looks different for each level of engagement:
- No enjoyment of the task + low relationship with the extrinsics for doing the task = non-compliance
- No enjoyment of the task + high relationship with the extrinsics for doing the task = compliance
- Enjoyment of the task + high relationship with the extrinsics for doing the task = interest
- Enjoyment of the task + low relationship with the extrinsics for doing the task = absorption

Engagement is about the task and how I feel about the task.

Engagement is not a synonym for fun. In fact, when we are at the highest level of engagement, i.e., absorption, we are working very hard on something that is challenging. We do so because we feel rewarded by our efforts. In fact, we would rather work on rewarding, challenging tasks (absorption) than boring, easy tasks (compliance). Why? Because engagement means we're doing something we want to do and are getting rewarded for our efforts. It is not rewarding to spend time working on tasks that require no effort.

> **In school, engagement means we are not simply trying to entertain students or ask them to do tasks where perfection is achieved at the first attempt.**

Engagement comes when we are working at the high end of our zone of proximal development (ZPD), and that means we're cognitively stretched; we are standing on our cognitive tiptoes, grasping at something that is within reach only if we are willing to put in the effort.

The problem is schools traditionally communicate feedback with grades and averages. And that's the worst thing we can do if we're aiming for engagement, because it means that perfection is the goal of each attempt. After all, if someone is working at the high end of their ZPD, they're going to fail. Rather than being avoided, failure should be celebrated, since it is critical to learning. However, if we grade everything and then average it all, then students will focus on the grade—not the learning. But instead of changing the way we grade, we end up changing the rigor of the tasks we assign. This leads to easier tasks so that students can get good grades. Ironically, that means we reduce the possibility for students to get engaged, since it is not rewarding to spend time working on tasks that require no effort. Thus, rather than creating "fun" tasks, we should create tasks that are aligned to *learning outcomes* in a manner that requires some level of challenge. In short, learning can be fun, but tasks that are fun are not always where learning happens.

> We do not do engagement activities because we think we do not have enough time. The problem is that if you do not engage students, you have wasted your time.

The difference between compliance (low-level disengagement) and interest (low-level engagement) is that students who are compliant do not want to do a task, whereas those who are interested do. So here's the challenge for teachers: How do you create tasks that students want to do? There's no doubt this is a question without a one-size-fits-all answer. What will work for one teacher won't work for another. This year's class is different from next year's. The students in your first period have a different response than the ones at the end of the day.

This is why we're sharing fifty strategies. Try one and see how it goes. If it works for you and your students, great! Use it and make it your own. If not, try another. There are plenty to choose from.

INSTRUCTIONAL DESIGN AND ENGAGING LEARNERS

TEACHING WITH THE 4 CS

Before diving into strategies using Google, we wanted to take a moment to highlight best practices regarding instructional design. After all, you can't Google Apps your way out of poorly designed lessons.

One best practice to incorporate into lessons is the 4 Cs. While there is nothing in this book that is a magic bullet, assignments and lessons that use at least one of the 4 Cs have a better chance of engaging students.

Creative Thinking

When students are all contributing the same answers or arriving at the same end result, they're not using creative thinking—and probably not critical thinking. Creative thinking does not have to be art; writing an essay can be a very creative endeavor! It can be very satisfying and indeed engaging for students to contribute their own ideas to coming up with a solution rather than following someone else's steps.

Collaboration

Cooperation and collaboration are not the same thing. Collaboration requires a degree of task switching so that the students interact with the work of other students. While students may complain about group work, especially when their grade is dependent on other students, the opportunity to work together to create something better than you could by yourself can be a source of student engagement.

Communicating Ideas

Have students go beyond providing steps, solutions, or filling out a graphic organizer. How did they arrive at the end result? What missteps did they make along the way? How will they communicate their thinking and the process? Communicating ideas is not only a way to combat cheating tools that provide students with solutions and summaries, it also allows students to demonstrate that they indeed were thinking about and engaged in a task.

Critical Thinking

A critical thinking task involves strategizing. "Hmm, I am not sure. Let me think about it."

If we expect that students will get the right answer the first time, what we've given them is probably not a critical thinking task. The opportunity to explore and figure things out provides students significantly more satisfaction than simply remembering a solution or process.

DEPTH OF KNOWLEDGE

Depth of Knowledge (DOK) is a four-point scale to indicate how much critical thinking a student is engaged in.

DOK 1	DOK 2	DOK 3	DOK 4
- Recall - Memorize - Follow an algorithm	- Skill - Application	- Strategic thinking - Justifying a claim with evidence	- Complex reasoning - Applying learning to a new situation

In short, DOK is about the mental complexity required to do the task, not about the difficulty of the task. For example, if you are not from Venezuela, asking you to name the capital of Venezuela might be difficult even thought the DOK level is 1 (since the question requires only simply recall). On the other hand, imagine a teenager asked you why crop tops are not appropriate for school. On face value, the question is easy. However, answering the question requires justifying your response with evidence, which is a DOK level 3.

It's important to note the DOK level does not create the engagement. For example, a gamified vocabulary activity on Quizizz is DOK 1 and can have high levels of engagement for a student—especially if the Quizizz activity has some novelty to it. Conversely, students who are assigned an argumentative essay (DOK 3) may not want to write an essay, and so their engagement in the task is low. Therefore, it's important to note a higher DOK task *may* increase student engagement because the student is interested in overcoming the challenge, but higher DOK levels are not a silver bullet for engagement.

5 ES LESSON PLAN MODEL

The 5 Es lesson plan model breaks away from the I do / we do / you do model. Instead, using the 5 Es means starting a lesson with students doing the thinking and exploring before you dive into explaining.

Engage

The first step in the 5 Es lesson plan model is to engage students. In some lesson plan models, this may be described as the "hook."

Simply throwing information at students will rarely lead to student engagement. First consider how will you design an experience that involves students being interested in learning the topic. This may be an interesting essential question, a prop, or an engaging video. Allow students to explore a concept before explaining it to them. Thinking is engaging. It is satisfying to try to figure things out. Provide students an opportunity to hypothesize, discuss, debate, research, simulate, or use manipulatives. In short, start the lesson with a hook that will entice the students to want to learn more about the topic.

Explore

In the explore phase, students get hands-on with the lesson's subject. They might work in pairs or small groups to tackle challenges that let them see trends and connections within the material. The teacher provides tools and activities that guide them to ask questions, test their ideas, and see the results. Exploring helps students start to understand the bigger picture themselves, which makes learning more meaningful and prepares them for the next steps in the lesson plan.

Explain

Ideally, the explain stage of the 5 Es lesson plan model has *students* explaining the concept. However, if they were not able to derive the information, a full-on direct instruction lesson may be warranted. By allowing students the opportunity to explore the concept first—even potentially unsuccessfully—you will get them more interested in gaining help in understanding from the teacher. Now they have invested effort into the task and want to know the answer.

Extend

Extend the lesson with an assignment, practice, or project. Students need practice. However, this does not necessarily mean homework. The location of practice is not the key.

Retrieval practice is more effective than homework. Frequently ask students to recall past information during class. Another method is to shift the practice time to the start of class the next day. This gives brains time to rest and allows students to revisit the learning from the previous day. Spaced repetition is more effective than intense practice. Regardless of how you have students practice, they need to interact with the material after the lesson.

Evaluate

How do you know if or what the students learned? Evaluation does not need to be a traditional multiple-choice test. You may evaluate that a student has learned through a conversation. Students may give an individual or group presentation. Or you can evaluate they have learned the material by observing their application of it in a different assignment.

USING THIS BOOK

Think of this book more like a recipe book than a novel. Turn to any page for an engagement strategy to try. The tips are color-coded and labeled according to the quadrants in the Engagement Matrix

1. **Non-compliance to Compliance:** Strategies that aim primarily to change the consequence or the relationship (yellow)
2. **Compliance to Interested:** Strategies that aim primarily to change the task (green)
3. **Interested to Absorbed:** Strategies that aim primarily to shift the motivation from extrinsic to intrinsic (blue)

The following table lists each strategy by number and shows which specific quadrant on the Engagement Matrix it's meant to move a student's engagement level into.

You will see that most of the strategies are ones that aim to help get students into the Interested quadrant. We need to celebrate interest, because it *is* engagement. Absorption, though it's the highest level of engagement, is not possible for all students for all lessons for all classes every day. Rather, our goal should be to ensure that all students are interested in all lessons for all classes every day AND to find ways for students to explore what is absorbing to them in school and bring experiences from outside of school to their learning.

At the same time, this is not just a how-to book that simply gives step-by-step directions on how to use a strategy. We wanted to include more than just the *how* but also some information on *what* and *why*. It is important to note that these strategies are not magical solutions. Instead, they are big ideas to consider when designing your lessons. The implementation of any strategy will depend on the unique conditions of your classroom, which we cannot control nor predict. Therefore, we suggest that you view our categorizations as suggestions rather than absolute rules. It is possible that a strategy we suggest to encourage compliance may actually increase student engagement for you, or vice versa. Similarly, a strategy that we suggest for generating interest may only result in compliance from your students. Our labels and organization were chosen based on what made the most sense to us, but we encourage you to reclassify them based on your own experiences, knowledge, and circumstances. We hope that these strategies will inspire you and provide a starting point for your own ideas and creativity in engaging your students.

One last note: Some technical applications of utilizing Google Apps to engage students are difficult to explain in the limited space of the book, so we've created a web page with additional tutorials for some of the concepts here. You can find these additional materials at alicekeeler.com/engagementbook using the passcode aliceheather.

For most of the engagement strategies listed in this book there is a sample or template. These templates are shared in a Google Drive folder at tinyurl.com/googleengagementfolder.

The 50 Ways to Engage Students with Google Apps

NON-COMPLIANT

✗

INTERESTED

1. Breaking Patterns
2. Interacting with Readers
3. Using Active Learning
4. Offering Choices
5. Scratching the Mystery
6. Reducing Participation Anxiety
7. Sorting for Critical Thinking
8. Jumping to Feedback
9. Encouraging Group Discussion
10. Choosing from Categories
15. Choosing the Questions
17. Recording Text Feedback
20. Targeting for All, Most, Some
23. Noticing and Wondering
24. Hyperlinking Google Slides
25. Earning Badges
26. Checking for Feedback
29. Forming Groups
32. Rebranding with Gamification
33. Creating with Pixel Art
36. Aiming for Mastery
37. Assessing the Standards
39. Integrating Peer Feedback
43. Embarking on Quest Chains
44. Choosing Adventure
45. Discovering Google Arts & Culture
46. Using Single-Point Rubrics
47. The Value of a Field Trip

COMPLIANT

12. Checking for Fluency
18. Focusing on the Product
19. Replacing Assignments
21. Checking In and Out
30. Personalizing with Names
31. Rethinking Learning Loss
34. Celebrating Success through Calls Home
35. Building Small Wins
40. Sharing in the Stream
50. Collaborating via Email

ABSORBED

11. Constraining Options
13. Fostering a Low Risk of Failure
14. Creating Clubs
16. Incorporating Personal Interests
22. Tracking Growth
27. Connecting with Authentic Audiences
28. Hosting Virtual Parent Meetings
38. Rethinking Grading
41. Tapping into Student Expertise
42. Showing Growth with Student Portfolios
48. Designing Collaborative Websites
49. Coding

50 Ways to ENGAGE STUDENTS with Google Apps

1. Breaking Patterns

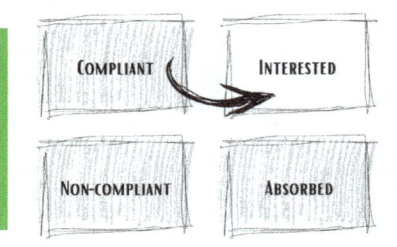

In school, we teach kids to be compliant. We tell them, "Do this work and you will get a good grade because we (the teachers) will make it so that you won't struggle. You can't struggle, in fact, because there is a grade attached to this work." But that's not what learning is like outside of school. Learning is messy and riddled with trial and error—but no grades. In fact, outside of school, learning is both about the product (the thing you're trying to do) and about the process (what you learn through the pursuit of the product).

Unfortunately, when we create environments where learning in school looks like learning outside of school—no grades and lots of messy trial and error—students may resist. They've been taught to focus on the product only, and they can shut down, push back, and dislike things when they are also being asked to focus on the learning process. This is because we have taught them process doesn't matter. Further, we implicitly teach them to be compliant and we reward that compliance. The "game of school" hinders us from moving students from compliant to interested. When students are stressed about getting a good grade, they become risk averse, which gets in the way of their learning.

Help students see that making many attempts at something is encouraged and part of the learning process. Provide them with a challenge they cannot likely complete correctly without multiple attempts. In other words, to break the pattern of classroom expectations, shift from focusing on the learning *product* to the learning *process*.

Google Slides can help students demonstrate the multiple attempts they've made in their work. Structure a template to indicate "first attempt," "second attempt," etc. Make it clear to students that you are looking for their learning process, not necessarily the end product. In fact, you may provide full credit for a task even if the student does not solve the problem yet has demonstrated perseverance and that they've approached solving the problem multiple ways.

In traditional classroom tasks, students simply need to repeat what they've heard or read. There is an immediate right or wrong answer. The answers are graded. Let's break the patterns so students have space to learn through repeated attempts in challenging opportunities.

TEMPLATE

Try an activity such as the provided five-piece puzzle template. The template is created in Google Slides to allow students to show multiple attempts using the multiple slides in the presentation. Slides also allows students to rotate the shapes with the rotation handle. Ask students to add shapes or text boxes in the slide to indicate their strategy or show their thinking about why they need to try something different.

tinyurl.com/5-Piece-Puzzle

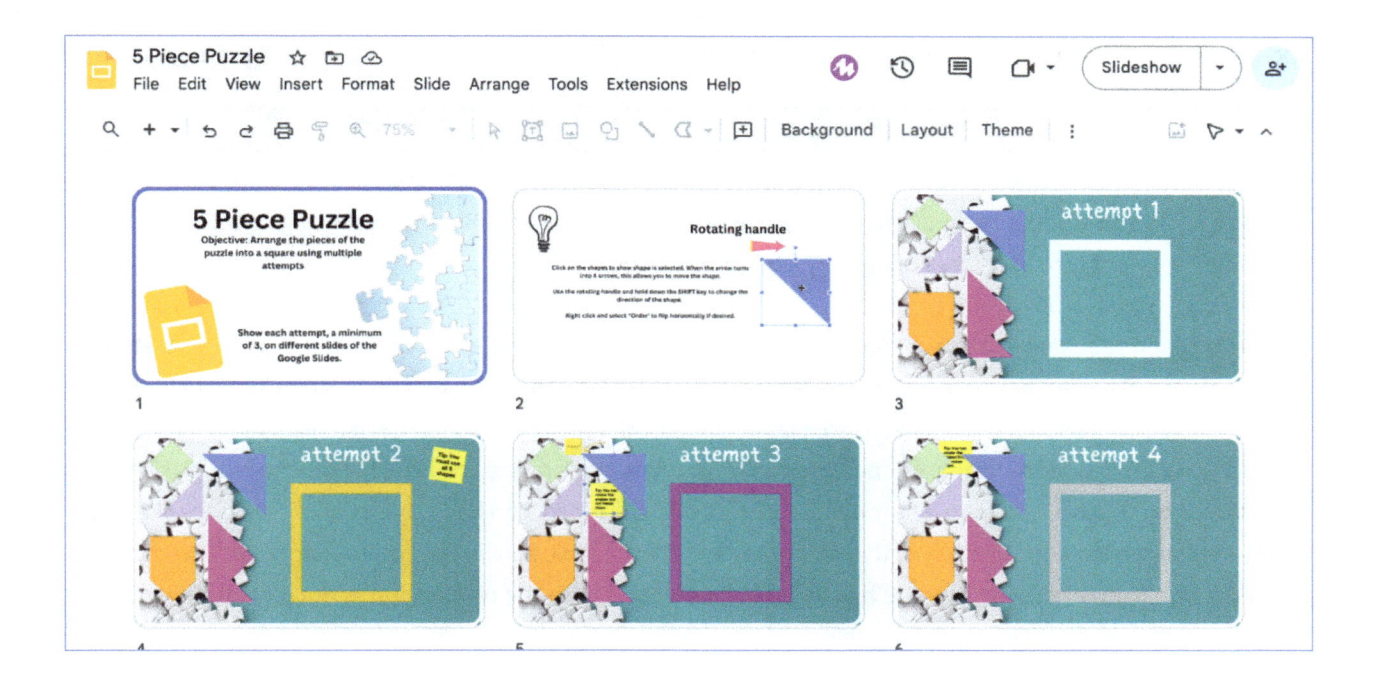

The purpose of using the Breaking Patterns strategy in this way is to expose students to the following concepts:

1. It's okay to not get it right the first time.
2. Perseverance through struggle.
3. Learning occurs through trial and error.

2. Interacting with Readers

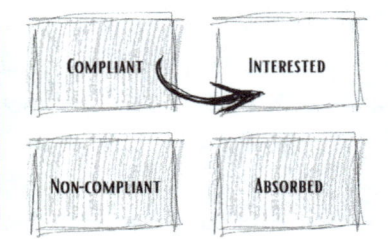

Even someone who doesn't like to read may find one book that they like. And if they do, they might become more interested in reading another book. This is the concept of momentum. Sometimes, all it takes to get a ball rolling is a little push.

Traditionally, reading logs have been used to encourage students to read. However, they can have the opposite effect. Logging is about compliance and may inadvertently shift students' focus from truly understanding and enjoying the material to merely finishing tasks so that they can fill in their logs. This can discourage deep learning and critical thinking, as students might prioritize meeting numerical goals over genuinely engaging with the content.

Students who are engaged when they're learning will have positive associations with learning; the opposite is also true. When students associate reading with tedious tasks rather than a genuine engagement with the text, they may enjoy reading less once they get out of school.

There is much research that says reading logs demotivate readers. That said, creating accountability regarding what students read is worthwhile. But logging is not the only way to achieve accountability for reading. The important aspect of reading accountability is that the reader needs to have interactions with others regarding what was read. Those interactions can be in the form of questions like "Tell me more about this" or "What do you think will happen later because of this event?" It can also be in the form of feedback like "You really understand the motivation of this character" or "Your prediction is very interesting! I can't wait to see if you're right!" In other words, there has to be an interaction with the reader that is not just students filling out a form to show they've read something.

Have students explain what they felt about the reading in a Google Doc. This should go beyond a summary of what they read. Instead, ask students to make connections to their reading. Have students utilize the VOICE-TYPING feature in the TOOLS menu to allow them to communicate ideas that might be above their reading level.

Google Sheets is an often overlooked tool for teaching reading. An advantage to using the collaboration features in Google Sheets is the creation of multiple tabs. Students can essentially create a reading notebook where they discuss what they read each day.

To use Google Sheets to engage students with their reading, make rows taller, columns wider, and set WRAPPING in the FORMAT toolbar to WRAP. This provides students ample space to share what they are thinking. Take advantage of Google Sheets's ability to organize information into tables to provide students with sentence stems for thinking about their reading rather than simply summarizing. To create larger feedback boxes, you can merge cells. This will give you more space to add comments and show that you are interested in what the student is reading. You can do this by selecting the cells you want to merge and then clicking on the MERGE CELLS button in the toolbar. You can also use the keyboard shortcut Ctrl+Shift+J to merge cells.

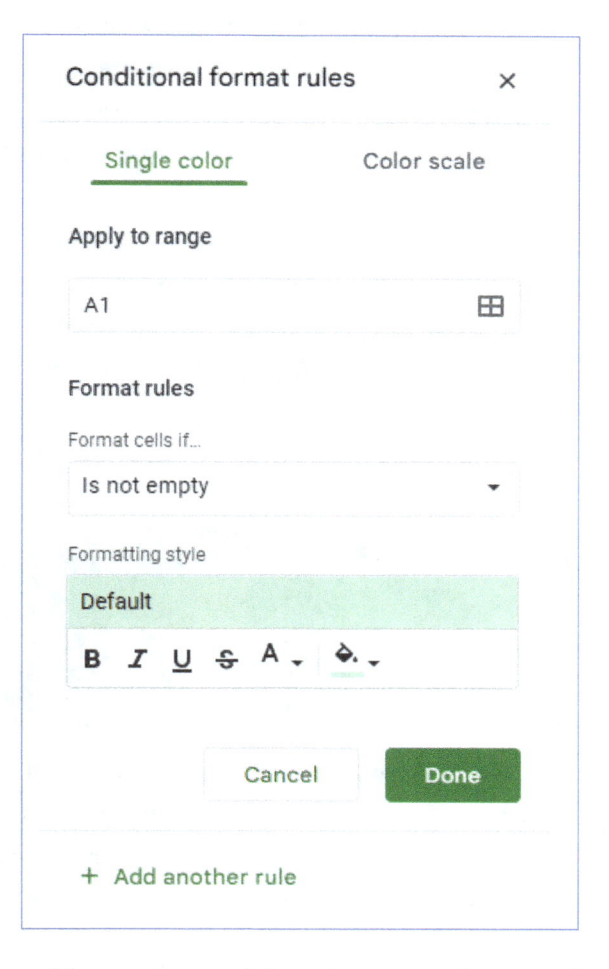

Utilize the knowledge you've gained from the shared file to engage students in conversations about their reading. When students know that you are paying attention, their motivation increases, and that can lead to deeper levels of engagement.

The purpose of using the Interacting with Readers strategy in this way is to expose students to the following concepts:

1. Accountability can be engaging.
2. Enjoying learning is motivating.
3. Interactions with readers increase authenticity.

> **TEMPLATE**
>
> Talking with students about their reading can help increase student interest in it. When students create a picture, they can feel pride in their image and enjoy sharing their creative endeavor with others. In the Engagement Picture Log activity, students are able to utilize the Pixel Art strategy later in this book to create a picture about what they read. In addition, students can put how they felt about the reading into a merged cell.
>
> Teachers are able to quickly engage with students when they open the shared Google Sheets to see an image. It is easier to get excited and have a conversation with a student about their reading when it includes a picture. Optionally, a merged cell is provided for the teacher to leave comments and feedback for the student on their pixel image and text.
>
> tinyurl.com/engagementpicturelog

3. Using Active Learning

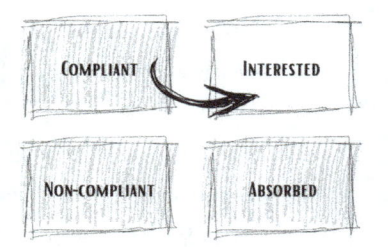

If you wanted to learn how to play a game, would you prefer to read the directions by yourself or have someone explain the game to you with words and actions? If you wanted to learn how to make your grandma's famous sauce, would you want to read her recipe and try to do it on your own, or would you prefer to be in the kitchen with your grandma so she could model what she does and support your attempts?

Most people prefer to learn from and with others. This is true when the others are peers who are also new to the experience, since the playing field feels leveled, and it is true when the others are more experienced with the task and able to guide the newbies. Finally, it is also true when the others are less experienced with the task, because then people can feel empowered by their ability to help those in need.

Active student engagement plays a crucial role in enhancing the learning process, leading to better understanding and retention of the material being taught. Harvard Professor Eric Mazur has done extensive research on peer instruction. His research emphasizes the significance of engaging students in their learning actively, as opposed to passive, lecture-based instruction. Actively engaged students are more likely to be motivated, curious, and invested in their education, resulting in deeper comprehension and longer-lasting knowledge. One of the key findings from this research is that active learning strategies, such as discussions, hands-on activities, and collaborative problem-solving, encourage students to actively process and apply new information. This active engagement stimulates critical thinking and promotes the development of essential cognitive skills. Furthermore, it fosters a sense of ownership in students over their learning experiences, leading to increased self-efficacy and self-regulated learning. As students become more involved in the learning process, they develop a stronger connection to the material, which translates to improved academic outcomes and overall learning experiences.[1]

When we learn together, we learn more.

Instead of having each student work on an individual Google Doc, consider having all students together in Google Slides. Create a single Google Slides where students have edit access. Each student adds a slide to the Google Slides. They can add their name to speaker notes below the slide.

> **TIP: You can find student work by using Ctrl+F to find their name.**

It can take some consistent uses of collaborative Google Slides to have a smooth activity experience. Students are not born knowing how to collaborate on digital documents. Just as we must patiently teach students how to walk to the library, we must teach them how to work in collaborative digital environments.

Use the students' work to guide discussions with the class. Students can insert comments on each other's work to "critique the reasoning of others" or to provide suggestions.

The purpose of the Using Active Learning strategy in this way is to expose students to the following concepts:

1. Learning is a cognitive process that occurs in a social setting.
2. No matter whether you're inexperienced or an expert with a task, when given the opportunity to work with others, everyone can benefit.
3. Learning through modeling improves real-time understanding.

> **TEMPLATE**
>
> Install the "Randomize Slides by Alice Keeler" add-on for Google Slides. This will allow students to collaborate on a single Google Slides and then have the responses shuffled to a random order.

---

1 Peter Reull, "Lessons in Learning," Harvard Gazette, September 4, 2019, https://news.harvard.edu/gazette/story/2019/09/study-shows-that-students-learn-more-when-taking-part-in-classrooms-that-employ-active-learning-strategies/.

4. Offering Choices

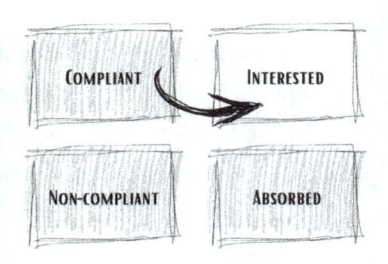

It's difficult to find the willingness to do something when you know it is too hard for you. If you have a broken leg and are wearing a cast, the idea of running a ten-yard dash is laughable. At the same time, if you are a marathon runner and you're told to run a ten-yard dash, you might also laugh. You can run for hours, so you might opt out of running such a short distance if the task is framed as "building stamina." In either case, you might be seen as non-compliant, but there's more to it.

The first question we need to ask when someone is being non-compliant is whether or not the task they're supposed to be doing is within their zone of proximal development (ZPD). If the task is too easy, the person will refuse it due to disinterest. If the task is too hard, the person will refuse to complete the task due to discouragement.

When thinking about ZPD, we can imagine a staircase: In order to get to the higher stairs, people need to first use the lower stairs. Considering this, teachers can create tasks that are:

- On step, for those students who are learning at the "expected" level;
- Below step, for those who are not yet at the "expected" level and need the point of entry lowered
- Above step, for those who are beyond the "expected" level and need the point of entry raised.

In schools, we usually give students one-size-fits-all assignments even when we know that the range of abilities in the classroom is not singular. It's no wonder that some students are non-compliant—the tasks they are being assigned are too easy in some cases and too hard in others. If some students cannot read at grade level, then choices to read on grade level will exclude them from success.

Google Forms are a great way to hear from students so you can get them on the right step. Create a Google Form with multiple sections for different leveled choices. A Google Form like this allows you to see what the student chose and help guide students with their choice.

Start by identifying a variety of tasks that will allow for every student to participate, then set up sections within the Google Form for each of the tiered choices. Within the sections, describe the choice and how the student will accomplish it. Google Forms allows for descriptions to be added to the sections with hyperlinks to a Google Doc or other source for additional directions on the choice.

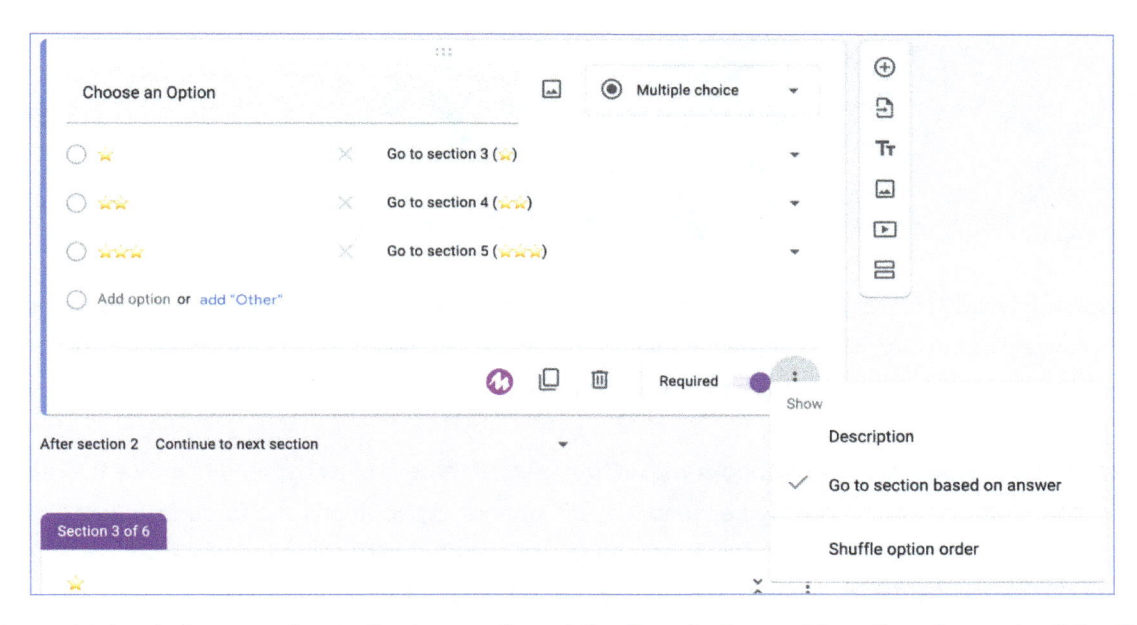

Add a multiple-choice question to the top section of the Google Form with options for each of the tiered choices. Be sure to enable branching for the multiple-choice question. Do this by using the three-dots menu on the question to GO TO SECTION BASED ON ANSWER.

Using this approach enables you to maintain a consolidated record of the students' selections. This not only simplifies the process of tracking their choices, it also allows you to swiftly assess who has chosen what before they commence their chosen task. If, based on your rapport with a student, you believe that an alternate option would be more advantageous, engage them in a discussion to explore why they might want to consider a different choice.

The purpose of using the Offering Choices strategy in this way is to expose students to the following concepts:

1. Self-efficacy impacts motivation.

It also allows teachers to:

1. Maximize the likelihood that all students will be able to participate in the learning.
2. Asses which students are truly in need of below-, on-, and above-level tasks.

TEMPLATE

This Google Form template is structured to provide three choices for approaching the learning objective. The branching within the Form is already set up, allowing you to quickly offer tiered choices to students.

tinyurl.com/engagementzpd

5. Scratching the Mystery

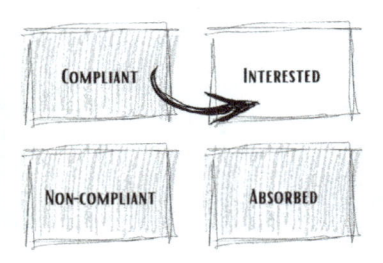

Neil Armstrong said, "Mystery creates wonder." Wonder is often a hook to help people become engaged. In fact, Armstrong's curiosity, which led him to walk on the moon, is the same curiosity babies tap into to learn to walk. Humans are naturally curious and drawn to wonder.

Curiosity is the reason authors write books with cliffhangers at the end of a chapter—to entice the reader to keep reading. Surprises are engaging because they disrupt our expectations and force us to pay attention. When we are surprised, our brains release dopamine, a neurotransmitter that is associated with pleasure and reward. This can lead to a feeling of excitement and anticipation, which can make us more likely to continue engaging with the thing that surprised us.

The Scratching the Mystery strategy feeds into the human desire to satisfy curiosity. Similar to lottery scratch off tickets, Google Slides can hide something behind an object. Students unlock the mystery by "scratching off" the top layer—deleting the shape—and revealing what is hidden beneath.

Unlike a traditional choice board, a Google Slides Scratchers choice board creates engagement through mystery. While this may feel like just a gimmick, the truth is this approach allows for student choice, unlike a traditional assignment, like a worksheet or end-of-chapter questions. In fact, with Google Slides Scratchers, you might assign different students different Scratchers, which means in addition to the choice the students have (which is differentiation), you could also have tiered options depending on the students' interests, readiness levels, etc. This way, the tool does more than just force compliance; it gets students to the interested level, which means they will be engaged.

To create a Scratcher, create a grid on a Google Slides. In each square, enter the question or assignment element. Create an image to go over the content on the slide. Students will delete the object to reveal what is below.

> **TIP:** Since it can be time consuming to create a grid of images to cover objects, create a generic grid of images. Use Ctrl+A to select all of the images on the slide and Ctrl+C to make a copy. Using Ctrl+V, paste the grid of images over the slide with the choices.

The purpose of using the Scratching the Mystery strategy in this way is to expose students to the following concepts:

1. Mystery makes the brain work harder, and intrigue builds engagement.
2. Learning is not one size fits all.
3. Disrupting expectations fuels engagement.

> **TEMPLATE**
>
> The Google Slides Scratchers template is an educational version of a lottery ticket scratcher. Students will "scratch off" (i.e., delete) the top image that hides the information/question/task behind it.
>
> Here is a link to a scratcher with math examples:
>
> **tinyurl.com/Engagement-Math-Scratcher**
>
> Here is a link to a scratcher with story elements examples:
>
> **tinyurl.com/Engagement-Story-Scratcher**
>
> Here is a link to a blank scratcher template:
>
> **tinyurl.com/Engagement-Blank-Scratcher**

6. Reducing Participation Anxiety

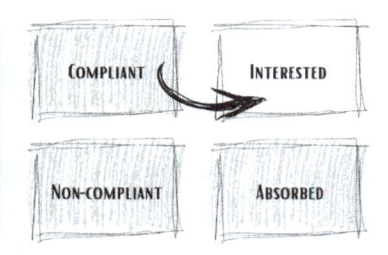

As teachers, we are constantly assessing what students know, both formally and informally. As we do so, we hope that we are getting an accurate picture of what they know. But anxiety and stress are deterrents to students demonstrating their knowledge. When put on the spot to answer quickly, students' brains may go into fight-or-flight mode, shutting down access to thinking. Therefore, rather than giving a sense of what they know, the students are showing how they feel—which can be perceived as them not being smart.

When students have time to collect their thoughts and respond, they are more likely to be able to demonstrate what they know.

Instead of calling on students randomly in class, ask all students to respond to the question on paper or in a digital format. Once all students have had an opportunity to think through and write down their response, randomly call on a student to share and elaborate on their response.

Digital tools can allow for all students to submit thoughtful answers. Provide students a Google Form to submit their response. In a connected Google Sheet, highlight the student responses and right click to select RANDOMIZE RANGE. This will allow you to select a few student responses to share with the class to further discussion.

Sharing collaborative Google Slides with the class gives each student the ability to add a slide and thoughtfully respond to a question. Use the "Randomize Slides" add-on to shuffle the student responses. Click on SLIDESHOW within Google Slides to display a randomly chosen response for the class to engage in discussion about.

The purpose of using the Reducing Participation Anxiety strategy in this way is to expose students to the following concepts:

1. Anxiety is reduced when thinking time is provided.
2. Participation doesn't always have to mean raising hands.

> **TEMPLATE**
>
> Create a new Google Form and use the "Popsicle Sticks by Alice Keeler" add-on.
>
> Post a question to the class and ask them to thoughtfully respond in the Google Form (keep your question generic since the form is reusable for any question you ask the class). Use the option to SHOW RANDOM RESPONSE to display a pop-up of a randomly chosen student and their answer. Read the answer aloud.

It also allows teachers to:

1. Improve classroom culture by asking everyone to participate before calling on students.

7. Sorting for Critical Thinking

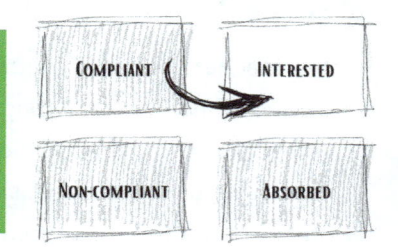

In *Classroom Instruction That Works*, Robert Marzano, Debra Pickering, and Jane Pollock note that identifying similarities and differences is a research-based strategy that improves learning. They point to comparing, classifying, metaphors, and analogies as examples of how to create similarities and differences for students.

Certainly, learning these processes can be done in a manner that is teacher directed and prescribed—"Here is the graphic organizer, fill it in." The level of engagement, however, is often minimized when we tell students what the pattern is that we want them to use.

Rather than being prescriptive and seeking a one-size-fits-all outcome, present students with the information and ask them to organize it in a manner that is meaningful to them. Doing so will create endless opportunities for students to show what they know. Put differently, having open-ended opportunities to model thinking requires students to be thinkers, and thinking is engaging.

While traditionally a presentation tool, Google Slides is very versatile as an interactive platform. It can be used to sort objects and words when you create text boxes or add images to a slide that students can drag around. Slides also allow students to add elements to help them communicate the patterns they notice in their sorting. Students can create Venn diagrams, draw organizational structures, or use lines to connect concepts that have elements in common.

The purpose of using the Sorting for Critical Thinking strategy in this way is to expose students to the following concepts:

1. Finding patterns.
2. There are multiple ways to approach the same set of information/data.

It also allows teachers to:

1. Create opportunities with "low floors" and "high ceilings."

> Tip: Use Ctrl+A on a slide to select all of the text boxes. Change the color, font, and font size all at once.

TEMPLATE

Install the "Seating Chart Slides by Alice Keeler" add-on for Google Docs. This allows you to take a list of words from a Google Doc and create a tile on a Google Slides with each word. To use the add-on, create a Google Doc with vocabulary words. Each word will need to be on its own line. Utilize the EXTENSIONS menu to select SEATING CHART SLIDES and send the terms to Google Slides. Each item is added to its own text box, ready for sorting.

8. Jumping to Feedback

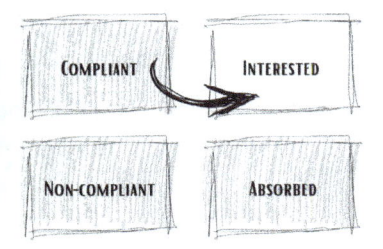

One of the most important jobs of a teacher in a classroom is to circulate and provide real-time feedback to students. Sometimes, the feedback reinforces what the students are doing—"You're on the right track! I like the way you're doing X, Y, and Z." Sometimes, the feedback is meant to course correct for students who might be heading down the wrong path: "Let me stop you and re-explain how to do this." Giving feedback can also help the teacher to better understand the students' thinking through questioning: "Can you help me understand what you're saying here? Tell me more about this."

While this can be done when a teacher is literally walking around the room, feedback can also be provided by circulating through students' digital work and providing digital comments in real time or before the next class. The point is that with teacher feedback as affirmation, correction, and/or questioning, students have a chance to validate and improve their work while it is in the formative stage. After all, it's not helpful to get feedback on something after it is due if you can't go back and apply the feedback. If you want to provide feedback between classes, consider giving students a feedback date instead of a due date.

You can even give live feedback while students are working on an assignment.

Open the folder in Google Drive that contains the students' documents and open multiple student documents from Drive in their own tabs. (Optionally, use the Drive20 Chrome extension to open multiple student documents at once.) Notice the icon at the top of the document indicating the student is actively working on the document. This is the COLLABORATOR icon. Clicking on it jumps you to the place in a document where the other person is at that moment. Insert comments near where the student is actively working on the file, using the keyboard shortcut Ctrl+Alt+M to insert comments. Cycle through documents while they are actively working to provide live feedback to more than one student.

The purpose of using the Jumping to Feedback strategy in this way is to expose students to the following concepts:

1. Real-time feedback allows for improvements during the learning process.
2. Learning is formative and iterative.

It also allows teachers to:

1. Increase the likelihood that feedback will be used to make improvements to current and future work.

> **TEMPLATE**
>
> Use the Jump to Feedback template provided when giving students a document per student. The icon in the header will help to remind you that you can click on the COLLABORATOR icon to instantly engage with the student while they are working.
>
> **tinyurl.com/engagementjump**

9. Encouraging Group Discussion

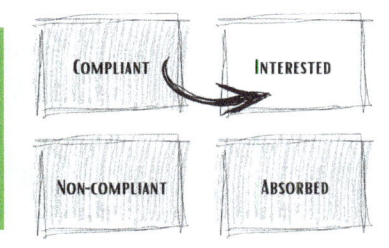

Having students participate in conversation can be really interesting. Under the right circumstances, students can be so into their conversation that they keep it going after the bell has rung on their way out of class. This is the hallmark of the highest level of engagement—absorption.

We are probably more familiar with less engaging pseudodiscussions, where the students do not really interact with each other and just wait until they are called on to answer questions from the teacher. If you have ever watched or participated in baseball or softball practice, you know that there are times when one child is up to bat and everyone else on the team is in a holding pattern watching the batter. The pitcher throws the ball and the batter swings as everyone else watches. Waiting. Swing. Miss. Pitch. Rather than engaging all the players at once, there is one player who is doing the work while the others watch and wait. Even in a game, after every pitch, the game can only proceed after the adult (umpire) comments.

Questions and discussions in a classroom can feel the same way. The teacher is the pitcher and lobs a ball out there. Sometimes it's to one student (the batter). Sometimes it's to the class (the field). One student answers and then throws the ball (the answer) to the teacher and the teacher catches it and throws out another ball (question). The teacher can be just as bored by this dynamic and wistfully hopes that some kid will "catch the ball."

Now, think of a soccer game where the children are all on the field passing the ball to each other, sometimes having the ball taken away by someone on the other team. The action is constant, and the adult only monitors the play and comments when needed—for example, when the ball has gone out of bounds or when a player violates a rule. A classroom discussion like this feels very different from the baseball-style discussion. The teacher might provide the class with the specs of the field (i.e., the topic for discussion), but the game is played only by the students. They question each other instead of going back and forth between the adult and one student.

Google Slides can be hacked for this kind of group collaboration and brainstorming. You can have one Google Slides per group that allows the students to structure their group discussion and each group member with an element of the discussion question to research. Students can use shapes, text boxes, and images on a slide to organize their research.

Then, on the slide, the students in groups combine what they discovered on a topic and create a group conclusion. This can eventually lead to a larger group discussion where students report on their conclusions or formalize their work in Google Slides.

The purpose of using the Encouraging Group Discussion strategy in this way is to expose students to the following concepts:

1. All students have equal opportunity and accountability to participate.
2. The collective intelligence of multiple people is greater than what any single person can achieve independently.

> **TEMPLATE**
>
> The Group Discussion template with Google Slides allows students to be grouped together. When the group communicates within the slides, all students are able to contribute.
>
> **tinyurl.com/Engagement-Group-Discussion**

It also allows teachers to:

1. Ensure that learning is done by the people doing the work. More people participating leads to greater learning for more people.

10. Choosing from Categories

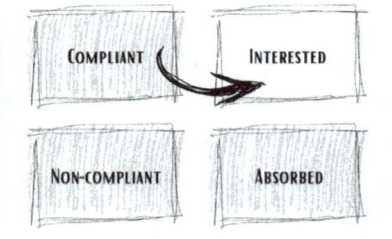

Imagine going to a restaurant where there was only one item on the menu. Most people would not want to go back. Why? People respond positively to options. Having too few choices creates a feeling of restriction. On the other hand, being given too many options creates a feeling of being overwhelmed. The goal is to offer just enough choices to create a feeling of personalization.

The Pick 5 choice board is really a choice board in which students choose five tasks from a variety of activities. It can be an effective tool to engage students because it offers both autonomy and differentiation, allowing students to take ownership of their learning experience. By providing students with a variety of categories and difficulty levels, the choice board caters to a diverse range of learning styles, abilities, and interests. This can lead to increased motivation, engagement, and a deeper understanding of the material.

Moreover, the structure of the Pick 5 choice board encourages students to challenge themselves by picking problems with varying difficulty levels. This not only promotes critical thinking and problem-solving skills but also helps build confidence as students tackle more complex tasks.

When making a Pick 5 choice board, remember to:

1. Create a choice board in Google Slides where students must pick from a variety of categories. Perhaps they will need to pick at least one easy, medium, and hard problem.
2. Design a layout for your choice board by creating separate sections for each kind of problem. You may want to use different colors, shapes, or text styles to differentiate between the categories.
3. In each category section, provide two or three options for students to choose from.
4. Be sure to include clear instructions and any necessary resources for each task.

In the Pick 5 template, there are only two or three options per category. Asking students to pick five allows them to choose which tasks or questions they want to tackle, but they can't choose only easy problems.

> Tip: Notice that many of the templates provided for this book "force" a copy. These types of templates automatically create copies of the original documents in the student's Google Drive that can be submitted through Google Classroom.
>
> Here's how you can force a copy of a template in Google Docs, Sheets, or Slides: Create a file for students to complete the task, then set the sharing permissions to Anyone with the link can view. Notice that the URL for your template it ends in /edit. There may be additional elements after the word *edit*. Remove the word *edit* and anything after it from the URL and replace it with /copy.

The purpose of using the Choosing from Categories strategy in this way is to expose students to the following concepts:

1. Students have choice in what they learn and how they learn it.

It also allows teachers to:

1. Create differentiated challenges.
2. Build a sense of ownership for students.

TEMPLATE

This Google Slides template is ready for you to add Easy, Medium, and Hard selections. Use the "Hyperlink Slides Choice Board" add-on in the EXTENSIONS menu. Choose TEXT ON SLIDES to create the linked choice pages.

tinyurl.com/Engagement-Choose-5

11. Constraining Options

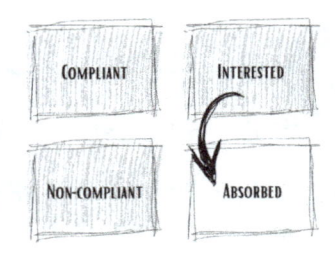

If the goal of golf were to simply get the ball in the hole by any means possible, players would walk the ball over to the hole and place it in every time. This would make for a very boring game. Instead, players must use a small stick to drive the ball into the hole without using their hands or feet to touch the ball. It's these constraints that make the game exciting.

Obviously, golf is not the only place where constraints come into play. All games have them, as do other facets of our lives. For example, we all have twenty-four hours in a day and we all have to eat. What we do with our time and the food we choose to eat is up to us.

In schools, we can use constraints to fuel engagement. This is because constraints can challenge us to think creatively and come up with innovative solutions. When we are faced with limitations or restrictions, we are forced to think outside of the box and find new ways to approach a problem or task. This can be especially motivating when we are able to overcome these constraints and achieve a successful outcome.

Constraints also encourage us to prioritize and focus on what's most important. With limited options or resources, we are forced to make strategic decisions. This can help us stay focused on our goals and avoid getting distracted by less important tasks or activities.

For example, consider Open Middle, a website that provides challenging math problems designed to encourage problem-solving, critical thinking, and creativity in students. These problems have a unique structure: they have a specific starting point and end point, but the middle part is open-ended, allowing for multiple pathways to reach the solution.

For example, consider this problem from OpenMiddle.com using the digits 1–9:

> Fill in the blanks with digits from 1–9, using each digit only once, to create a multiplication problem with the smallest possible product.
>
> ___ x ___ = ___

This problem has a clear starting point (filling in the blanks with digits from 1–9) and end point (creating a multiplication problem with the smallest possible product). However, there are multiple ways to approach this problem and reach the solution.

Create a list of constraints for your students. For example, for an ELA writing project, you might limit character traits or scene elements. For math it might be strategies for tackling a problem. Randomly assign students a subset of the constraints.

Giving each student their own subset of constraints not only minimizes the students' ability to copy off of each other, it makes the task more fun! Students can collaborate and brainstorm with each other yet produce their own unique end product.

You can create this list of constraints in Google Sheets then shuffle them by highlighting the list, right clicking, and selecting RANDOMIZE RANGE. Highlight the first few constraints and paste them into a Google Slides or a Google Doc.

The purpose of using the Constraining Options strategy in this way is to expose students to the following concepts:

1. Creative problem-solving can force individuals or teams to think outside the box and find innovative solutions to problems.
2. Needing to work together expands possible solutions.
3. Prioritization when working with restrictions.

> **TEMPLATE**
>
> Install the "Seating Chart Slides by Alice Keeler" add-on. Create a list of constraints in a Google Doc, then using the EXTENSIONS menu, choose the option CREATE MAGNETS. You will be prompted to enter how many constraints you wish each student to be provided. You will also be prompted to enter how many versions you'd like to create. This allows you to have a different list per student or group.

12. Checking for Fluency

When you go to a sporting event, both the audience and the athletes use the scoreboard to know how the game is going. The scoreboard helps to inform and also to motivate. Who doesn't like to know they're ahead?

Using the strategy Reading Racetrack by intervention expert Jim Wright, author of several books about the Response to Intervention approach and creator of the website www.InterventionCentral.org, Heather created the strategy Read for Speed for her youngest son when he had trouble with sight-word fluency. Here's how it works: First, listen to the student read and create a list of words that they have trouble with. Then enter five to eight of those words into a template and shuffle them. Once per day, the student is given the chart and asked to read as many words in order as they can within one minute. (It's critical to randomize the words so that the student has to really read the words rather than learn the pattern in the chart. To do so, highlight the list of words in Google Sheets, right click, and select RANDOMIZE RANGE.) Then note the number of words they read correctly and the overall number attempted. This is the time to review any missed words and to talk to the child about their score. This process is done once a day for a week.

A great way to help students check for fluency is to use checkboxes in Google Sheets or in Google Docs, which allow students to see progress toward goals. Create a list of goals for students in a Google Sheets spreadsheet and use the INSERT menu to insert checkboxes in the cells next to each goal. When the student is done with their tasks, highlight the checkboxes and use the spacebar to quickly select and deselect the list. This allows for quickly starting over.

The purpose of using the Checking for Fluency strategy in this way is to expose students to the following concepts:

1. Data are motivating.
2. Fluency comes through repeated exposure and practice.
3. Progress can be quickly noted.

> **TEMPLATE**
>
> Though this was originally created for sight-word fluency, it can be used in other content areas. Science teachers could use it with elements from the periodic table. Art teachers could use images from different artists or different periods in art history. The list is endless.
>
> After making a copy of the template, add a list of items to the second tab. Using the EXTENSIONS menu, install the "Select the Cells" add-on. One of the options in the menu is CHECK FLUENCY. Choosing PLACE WORDS will randomize the list. Test students' familiarity with the word or concept and check it off.
>
> Since random exposure helps to create permanency, be sure to throw in old words on new lists and/or keep a word that the student struggled with on next week's list.
>
> **tinyurl.com/engagementfluency**

13. Fostering a Low Risk of Failure

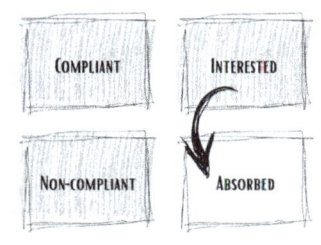

The purpose of school is to earn points and get good grades—at least, many students perceive it this way. Perceiving the purpose of an assignment as a means to an end (the grade), means students will be less engaged in the learning aspect of the activity.

In order to grow intellectually, students need to take risks in learning new things. However, students will be risk averse if they perceive that their efforts to try something new will be met with a lower grade.

Instead of making the correct answer the final criteria for a task, ask students to demonstrate their thinking and creativity. Even if students do not solve the challenge or come up with the "correct" solution, provide them FULL CREDIT for engaging in the task. Removing the threat of losing points allows students to reduce their anxiety and focus on the productive struggle.

Math teacher Diana Herrington did just this. She asked her students to choose any three problems from a text and complete them in Google Slides. The students would receive feedback from the instructor on these three problems. So long as the students responded to her feedback, the students would receive full credit. At first, all of the students would choose the easy problems from the text. However, the point of the assignment was not to do three problems. The point was to learn more. Herrington inserted comments onto the Google Slides with questions to help further develop students' thinking. Students then came back to the

Slides and updated their response. By the end of the semester, 100 percent of the students would choose the difficult problems. Once they were given a low risk of failure and rewarded with full credit for their efforts, students demonstrated that they truly wanted to go deeper in mathematical reasoning.

In Google Apps like Google Slides, the instructor and the student can have editing access to a document at the same time. Students do not need to submit work in order to receive feedback.

Assign each student a task in a Google Slides that is shared between the teacher and the student. This can be accomplished by using the MAKE A COPY FOR EACH STUDENT feature in Google Classroom.

After they've been given time to make initial attempts on the assigned challenge, go into each student's Google Slides and use the COMMENTING feature (Ctrl+Alt+M) to insert feedback comments. The feedback should be aimed at developing students as critical thinkers by posing questions to help students progress with the task. In other words, rather than giving feedback on whether or not the student is correct, help the student think through the quality of their response.

Ask students to not resolve the comments, but to respond to the comments with updates to their work.

Using the VERSION HISTORY feature or the COMMENT icon at the top of Google Slides, students and teachers can see recent feedback left in the Google Slides.

As long as the students make additional efforts in problem-solving and perseverance, reward them—even if they do not finish the challenge.

The purpose of using the Fostering a Low Risk of Failure strategy in this way is to expose students to the following concepts:

1. Focusing on the learning and not the grade.
2. Regardless of the initial or ultimate outcomes, trying something can be safe.
3. With repeated attention, the quality of their work will improve.

> **TEMPLATE**
>
> Use this Google Slides template to allow students to demonstrate their creative critical thinking. Make a copy for each student and provide them with actionable feedback to help them go further.
>
> **tinyurl.com/engagementpersevere**

14. Creating Clubs

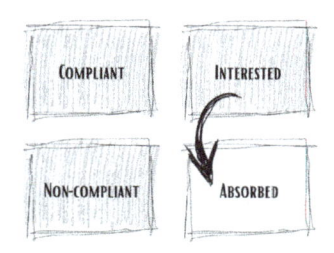

Not everyone wants to come to school to learn. While that may sound obvious, the question then becomes, What is engaging to those who may not be engaged in learning?

Create a club within your class that students can join. This creates connections with other students who are interested in the same topic. For middle school and high school teachers, these clubs can traverse class periods.

High school English teacher Barton Keeler created a book club within his class that students could choose to join. Members read *The Scarlet Letter* and had in-class discussions about the book—or they could instead engage with a different class assignment. While not all book selections were offered as a "book club," the occasional opportunity for choice led to increasing engagement for those students in the club.

Google Classroom is the perfect venue to provide club opportunities to students. Create a separate Google Classroom class just for a topic that a selection of students are interested in.

On the PEOPLE tab in Google Classroom, add the email addresses of the students who indicated they wanted to join the club. Alternatively, offer students the link or class code to join the club.

Google Classroom makes it easy for students to share thoughts and ideas about a topic in the class Stream. They can share pictures, resources, and post questions to club members.

Use the Google Classroom club as a way to provide students with another way to engage in your class, either through alternative assignment choices or simply as a way for students to connect with other students.

The purpose of using the Creating Clubs strategy in this way is to expose students to the following concepts:

TEMPLATE

This template provides several options for sharing the code to an optional Google Classroom. Printing out flyers to post around the room or school easily allows students to opt in and access information, permission slips, and activities exclusive to that group.

tinyurl.com/engagementflyer

1. Choice leads to deeper connections with learning.
2. They are more engaged when they are able to connect their interests to learning in school.
3. Not every student needs to do identical work to achieve the intended learning outcomes.

15. Choosing the Questions

All teachers assess students every day even if they don't know it. This is called *formative assessment*, or assessment to inform learning.

When we think about testing, we tend to default to standardization—meaning that all students have to answer the same questions to show that they know the same content. Certainly, there are times when standardized assessments should be given. However, this does not always have to be the case—particularly when trying to achieve engagement.

The idea for this strategy comes from author and consultant Brian Mendler.

When students answer questions, allow them to select which questions they would like to answer and which ones they can skip. Is there a way to allow students to choose seven of ten, for example, so they don't have to do all the parts? This is an easy method of differentiation since the teacher will likely be creating all of the questions anyway. Imagine the heightened engagement students will have when they feel like they are allowed to only do the seven easiest questions. But there is a lot of metacognition required of them to determine which questions to answer. Even if a student only does the first seven (and therefore does not take the time to assess which are the "easiest"), the fact is that the student is still doing the work.

Design sections in a Google Doc indicating that students can pick a single or selection of questions from the section, for example, "For this section, choose one of the three questions" or "In this section choose two of the five questions to respond to."

The default when typing in a Google Doc is NORMAL TEXT. This is visible in the toolbar next to the font style. Change

TEMPLATE

In the Google Docs assessment template, sections are created with directions for students to select a subset of the questions. Notice the checkbox in the section can be checked by clicking on it.

tinyurl.com/engagementchoicetest

the text style to HEADING 1 for each of the sections.

It is not unusual for a student to start a question but change their mind and their selection midway through an answer. Use the CHECKLIST style in the toolbar to help students clearly indicate which of the choices they are submitting.

The purpose of using the Choosing the Questions strategy in this way is to expose students to the following concepts:

1. Building relationships and rapport.
2. Personalization fortifies interest and commitment.
3. Creating opportunities for choice increases engagement.

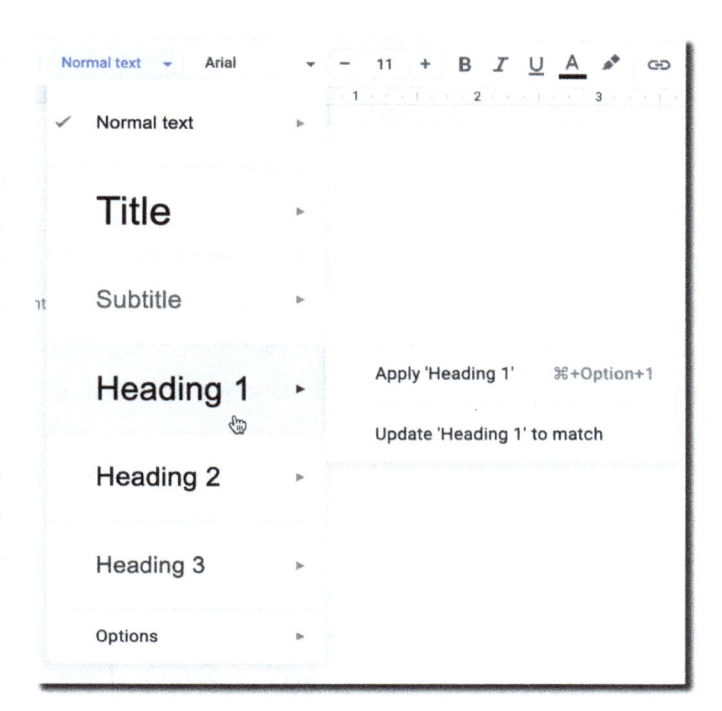

16. Incorporating Personal Interests

One of the many advantages of having a teacher rather than a canned-curriculum online course is that the teacher can incorporate their students' interests into lessons. If the students really enjoy hockey and the textbook contains an activity that students may not find interesting about surfing, the teacher can modify the lesson to incorporate hockey. While this example is very basic, the impact of integrating students' interests is not.

Everyone has an intense interest in something. Thus, perhaps rather than thinking that teachers need to create interest, we should think about how we can provide ways for students to link their interests to the learning in the classroom.

Here is what is important: We have yet to find someone who doesn't demonstrate absorption in at least one thing. It could be reading, playing a sport, hiking, some type of art or craft, cooking, playing a video game, playing an instrument, gardening, posting on social media, searching Pinterest, or learning a new language. The list is truly endless. As well, while human beings are interested in tangible things like people or places, they are also interested in ideas like discrimination or justice. You can tap into their feelings, like loyalty or humanitarianism. When you allow people to connect to the things they already care about, they are more likely to care about what you want them to connect to.

While you may not be able to help someone who is interested in dinosaurs find engagement in the French and Indian War, that does not mean that there are no other entry points for making connections. That same person may care a lot about colonization or North American conflicts or the plight of indigenous people. If we are only seeing interest as an opportunity to connect to specific things like hobbies, we say things like "Bella likes soccer, but there's no way to link soccer to what we're learning about." We'll give up too easily on finding ways to engage students at the highest levels. On the other hand, if we broaden our entry points to feelings and ideas, we exponentially increase the possibilities for absorption.

Seeking knowledge about others is not just important for building relationships, it is also a great way to understand what motivates others. When you understand student interests and motivations, you are able to better design tasks and learning environments that they will find engaging.

Design a Google Form to poll students on their interests and what captivates their attention. What do students find they get absorbed in? Strive to integrate their feedback when crafting lesson plans, and use examples that students can connect with instead of solely relying on defining concepts from the text.

The purpose of using the Incorporating Personal Interests strategy in this way is to expose students to the following concepts:

1. Having voice in how they learn.
2. Seeing first to understand.
3. Connections between what interests them and what they are learning.
4. Finding connections to others they are learning with.

TEMPLATE

The What Interests You Form shows samples of questions that delve into what students like in terms of *things* and *environments*.

tinyurl.com/engagementinterestsform

17. Recording Text Feedback

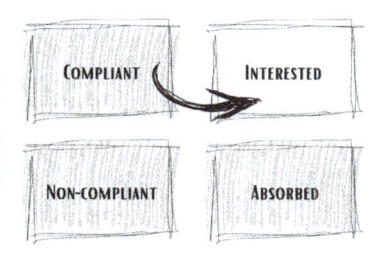

When we were students, it was common to have teachers provide feedback in red pen. Hence the cliché "Your paper is bleeding." Seeing marks all over their work can be quite intimidating or off-putting to some students.

Too much text—be it in feedback or in directions—can pose a challenge for students who are not yet able to read or some students with disabilities. If the student is at home or doesn't want to be pulled away from their peers, how can teachers accommodate students who need support with directions or feedback?

Digital recording tools can alleviate these issues! Adding your voice to the digital elements of your class can help all students better connect with the learning. The Mote Chrome extension allows you to record your voice and add the recording to Docs, Sheets, Slides, Forms, and Google Classroom, and it's COPPA and FERPA compliant. Adding your voice increases accessibility. It becomes easier for all students to engage with materials when accessibility is taken into consideration. The importance of students feeling that their teacher is present in their digital materials cannot be understated. Instead of cold text for students to interact with, Mote allows students to hear the warm tone of their trusted teacher.

Install the Chrome extension Mote. It allows you to record a quick "Mote note" and automatically copies the link to the recording to your clipboard. This allows you to paste the recording into your Google Classroom directions or anywhere you can post text.

The purpose of using the Recording Text Feedback strategy in this way is to expose students to the following concepts:

1. It can be easier to understand when directions are read and explained.
2. Feedback helps them grow.
3. Feedback doesn't have to be intimidating (like a red pen).

RESOURCE

Go to mote.com to learn more about the many features that Mote provides Google Workspace users. Install the Chrome extension and, if possible, have your tech department push Mote out to all of the student Chromebooks.

18. Focusing on the Product

Many adults use voice-to-text functions on their phones because it is faster and easier than typing with their thumbs. However, there is a stigma attached to using voice-to-text on computers. This is unfortunate, because voice-to-text can be a valuable tool for students and writers of all ages.

For those who find typing on a full-sized keyboard challenging, voice-to-text features can reduce the cognitive load on writers and allow them to concentrate on producing quality written content. Moreover, writing with text-to-speech technology can be particularly engaging, as it provides users with a more natural way to express their thoughts and ideas without the physical limitations of typing. In fact, voice-to-text can free students to focus on their ideas. This is especially beneficial for students who have difficulty typing or who have dyslexia.

By encouraging students to bypass the need for extensive keyboarding skills and instead focus on conveying their ideas through voice-to-text technology, educators can foster a greater sense of motivation and momentum in their students. Furthermore, text-to-speech software enables users to incorporate words and phrases that they may not be able to spell or write accurately but can still articulate effectively, thereby improving their overall writing ability.

Of course, there are some limitations to voice-to-text. The technology is not perfect and it can sometimes make mistakes, but this is why it's important to practice with it. As the user becomes more familiar with not just what they are saying but the commands they need to use, the process gets easier and improves the product.

In Google Docs, students can enable voice typing under the TOOLS menu. The keyboard shortcut Ctrl+Shift+S can also toggle voice typing for students.

Encourage students to start thinking through their ideas by using the voice-typing feature in Google Docs. Students can punctuate by saying "period" or "exclamation point." Saying "new line" will create a new paragraph within the Google Doc.

The purpose of using the Focusing on the Product strategy in this way is to expose students to the following concepts:

1. All students have equal opportunities to express their thoughts and ideas, which fosters a more inclusive learning environment.

It also allows teachers to:

1. Ensuring that all students have equal opportunities to express their thoughts and ideas, fostering a more inclusive learning environment.
2. Enable students to articulate their thoughts more quickly than typing or writing. This enables them to maintain a better focus on the task at hand and reduces the risk of losing their train of thought, ultimately leading to increased productivity and efficiency.
3. Reduce writing/typing anxiety.

> **TEMPLATE**
>
> Use the template to allow students to practice different techniques for voice typing in a Google Doc.
>
> **tinyurl.com/engagementpracticevoice**

19. Replacing Assignments

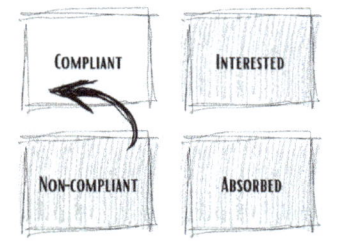

Some students may never be able to catch up when they get behind on work. This can create a scenario where students (a) know that no matter what they do now, they cannot pass and so (b) they stop trying. This does not help the teacher either, since students who do not have prerequisite knowledge will struggle with subsequent learning.

In reality, we know that doing something is better than doing nothing. With that in mind, how can you help a disengaged student to reengage? The easiest way to bolster engagement is to change the task. Rather than having the student complete all the back-work, provide them with one or more options to show the learning. Keep in mind, with this strategy, the grades for the alternative assignments do not have to be of equal value to the original assignments—here the goal is to achieve similar or equivalent *learning* to the original assignments.

Not only will this strategy lead to learning, it can also have a positive impact on your relationship with students. After all, showing the student you are committed to their success is a great relationship builder.

When a student has several assignments in Google Classroom they have not completed, create new assignments just for that student. When creating an assignment the default is ALL STUDENTS, so instead, deselect ALL STUDENTS and select only the intended student. For past assignments that are looming and feel overwhelming to the student, edit the assignment and remove the student from the list of students it is assigned to.

The alternative assignment may not be worth the same number of points and might likely be one assignment to replace multiple assignments.

The purpose of using the Replacing Assignments strategy in this way is to expose students to the following concepts:

1. There is always a possibility to show learning.
2. Bad starts don't have to lead to bad endings.
3. Learning is not time bound.
4. Success builds success.

> **TEMPLATE**
>
> Use the Assignment Forgiveness template to create a contract with a student around their missing assignment that says that if they complete the new assignment(s) by the due date, they will be excused from the missing assignments.
>
> **tinyurl.com/engagementreplacing**

20. Targeting for All, Most, Some

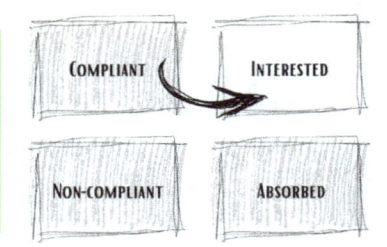

If you think about kids who are not doing work and appear to be non-compliant, it is worth noting that the reasons behind behavior can change over time. In other words, rebellious non-compliance is frequently due to an inability to do what is expected. A lack of skill can be hidden behind the mask of a lack of will. Some students would rather do nothing than look dumb. As you design activities, consider what every student can do so that all students have an entry point.

> If a student is not completing a task, is it really non-compliance or is it a mask for inability?

When planning your lessons, it's crucial to account for the standards and what is expected of all students. However, not all students commence their learning journey from the same point. To address this, consider utilizing a lesson-planning template on a Google Doc that includes a reflection on each student's abilities. This deliberate approach to designing learning experiences tailored to your students' needs can enhance the success of your class. It doesn't mean altering the standards but rather thoughtfully planning the journey to meet those standards based on each student's unique starting point. While lesson plans from book publishers, internet teachers, or instructional coaches can be helpful, they don't account for the specific students in your class.

This strategy is meant to provide all students a starting point that will allow them to be successful by creating tiered learning targets (see figure 5).

- The *All* learning target is written below level and is one that all students will be able to do.
- The *Most* learning target is written on level and aligns to the information that the students are currently learning.
- The *Some* learning target is written above level and is for students who are ready for more advanced ways to show their knowledge/skill beyond what the class is currently learning about.

Here's an example of this kind of learning targets and a straightforward rubric to use with them.

Figure 5

All	All students will list all the simple machines and give an example of each.
Most	Most students will identify how two simple machines work together and how this synergy improves what either could do independently.
Some	Some students will draw their own invented machine that solves a problem and includes at least two simple machines.

	A Student at This Level Will . . .			
	Struggling	Developing	Proficient	Highly Proficient
Accurately Complete Learning Target	No	Yes, but only the All	Yes, but only the All & Most	Yes, the All, Most & Some
Teacher Support Needed	For the All Portion	For the Most Portion	For the Some Portion	No Teacher Support Needed
Student Proficiency Level	1	2	3	4

The purpose of using the Targeting for All, Most, Some strategy in this way is to expose students to the following concepts:

1. All students should have the chance to show what they know—including those who may struggle and those who are ready for enrichment.
2. The person doing the work should give thought to what they can do and where they are still growing.
3. Learning is not one size fits all.

TEMPLATE

tinyurl.com/engagementallmostsome

> "If you are complaining about your students, change your lesson plans."
>
> —Alice Keeler

21. Checking In and Out

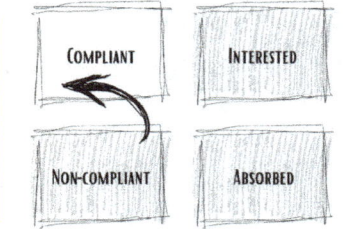

Check In/Check Out (CI/CO) is a Tier 2 intervention used in a Multi-Tiered System of Supports (MTSS) for students who need additional levels of connection and accountability. The connection comes from students working with a team of adults, including but not limited to teachers, student support personnel, administrators, and/or parents. Accountability comes from what the student and their team work on. Specifically, in collaboration with the student, the team identifies behavioral goals the student should achieve and positive rewards that the student will earn as a result of achieving the goals.

Basically, a plan is created with a small number (approximately three) of behaviors that you want to see more of. These are included in a tracking sheet that the student is responsible for.

When creating CI/CO, it's important to involve the child and even the child's parent/guardian. This deepens the feelings of investment and builds relationships. After all, you will be rewarding the child when they are successful at achieving the targeted behaviors, so you will need to develop rewards that are motivating to the child. As well, it's important to focus on the positive growth of the child, who may have some setbacks along the way.

It's also important to consider who the child will be checking in and out with. The CI/CO adult tends to be someone neutral who is not the child's teacher or anyone who is filling out the daily CI/CO form; it is the person who is reviewing the form with the student.

Creating a Check In/Check Out (CI/CO) intervention sheet can be done in a few steps within Google Sheets.

Create a table with the following columns: Date, Behaviors, CI/CO, and Rewards. The Behaviors column should list three or fewer behaviors that the student needs to focus on and that the team wants to see more of. The Rewards column should list the incentives agreed upon by the student and their support team.

Share the Google Sheet with the student and their team, including parents or guardians. Ensure that the student is responsible for updating the CI/CO columns each day to track their progress. The CI/CO columns serve as a way for the student to report their progress, and for the team to monitor and adjust the intervention plan as needed.

To share the Google Sheet, click on the SHARE button located in the upper right corner of the screen. Enter the email addresses of the team members who need access to the sheet, and select the level of access that you want to give them. If you are working with a large team, you can also create separate tabs in the sheet to keep the information organized.

Finally, schedule regular review meetings with the student and the CI/CO adult to discuss the student's progress and adjust the intervention plan as needed. These meetings provide an opportunity for the team to assess the student's progress and make any necessary changes to the intervention plan to ensure its effectiveness.

By utilizing Google Sheets to track the student's progress, the team can easily monitor and adjust the plan to focus on positive growth. Creating a CI/CO plan that is tailored to the student's needs and preferences can help to ensure that the student feels invested in the intervention, leading to better academic and social outcomes.

TEMPLATE

The Check-In/Check-Out template is an easy way for multiple adults (including teachers, support services, administrators, and family members) to have access to the student's goals and progress. Use the "TemplateTab" add-on in the EXTENSIONS menu to duplicate the daily template within the same spreadsheet.

tinyurl.com/engagementcheckin

The purpose of using the Checking In and Out strategy in this way is to expose students to the following concepts:

1. There are people in your life that care about you and are here to support your success.
2. Having a method to track success keeps the goal at the top of mind.
3. Visual methods make progress monitoring easy to see and do.

22. Tracking Growth

Imagine if you played a game but didn't keep score. If you were just trying to learn the rules of the game, that would make sense. After a while, though, even if you were playing without formally keeping score, you would start to wonder how you're doing and likely start to keep track on your own. Why do we want to know the score? Because knowing how we're doing helps us to think about what changes, if any, are needed.

Even children who are enrolled in town soccer leagues or peewee football keep score. Keeping score not only helps the players and coaches understand how the players are developing, it also gives them feedback to use to inform practices. If this is true for low-stakes games, it makes sense that this would also be true when the stakes are higher—like student learning.

In John Hattie's book *Visible Learning*, he identifies over 250 influences on student achievement and indicates the effect size of these influences on student outcomes based on a meta-analysis of tens of thousands of research studies on millions of students. According to Hattie's work, the effect size determines the effectiveness of the action, with effect sizes of greater than 0.4 being those that accelerate learning. What's more, Hattie identified nine strategies that emphasized student metacognition and self-regulated learning. Of those nine, all of them are above a 0.4, including "evaluation and reflection" (0.75) and "strategy monitoring" (0.58)—both of which connect to the concept of students charting their growth. Under the heading "Strategies emphasizing learning intentions," "learning goals vs. no learning goals" (0.68) and "cognitive task analysis" (1.29) also show strong impact on student learning. In short, having students set goals and monitor their progress in achieving those goals is not just engaging, it's educationally impactful.

As part of your classroom routine, give students time to chart goals that you have as a class.

Create a graphic organizer in Google Sheets, for example, and make a copy for each student. Include the goals or benchmarks that students need to meet. Seeing positive growth is engaging! Adding conditional formatting that shows students that they are making progress increases student engagement around tracking their own progress.

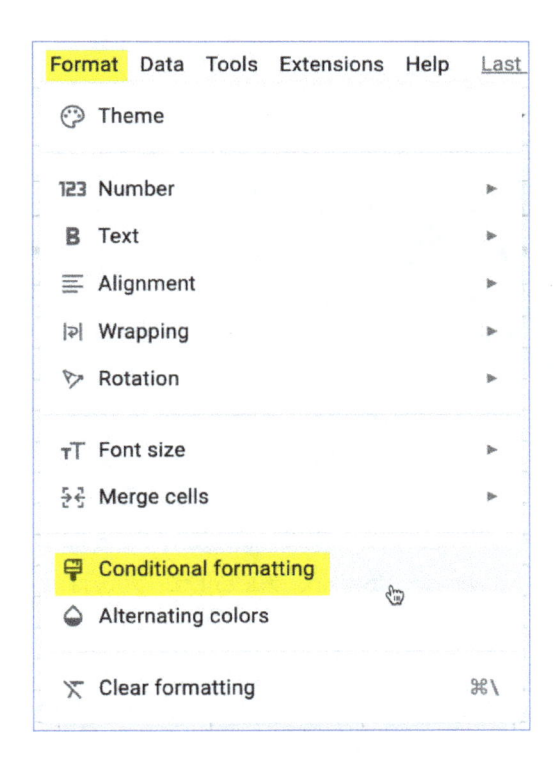

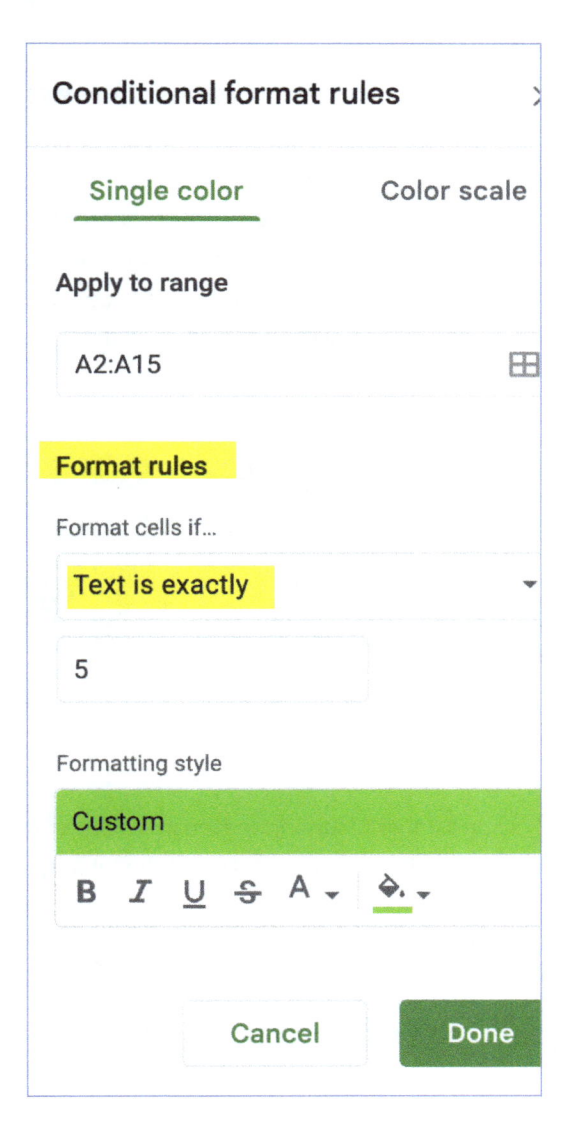

To add conditional formatting, highlight the values you want to highlight when students make certain benchmarks. Either use the FORMAT menu or right click to select CONDITIONAL FORMATTING. Under FORMAT RULES, choose the rule that suits the goal. For example, there is a rule called TEXT is exactly, which changes the color of the cell if the contents of the cell have the exact text you entered. Another example is the rule GREATER THAN, which changes the color of the cell if the numbers in the cell are greater than the minimum number you entered into the rule. These kinds of rules create immediate visual feedback for students.

The purpose of using the Tracking Growth strategy in this way is to expose students to the following concepts:

1. Having a method to track success keeps the goal at the top of mind.
2. Data are motivating.
3. Goals should focus on intrinsic growth and learning rather than extrinsic grades.
4. Progress monitoring allows for celebrations of growth and/or interventions due to regression or stagnation.

> **TEMPLATE**
>
> Our sample progress tracker allows you to list the standards or goals for students. Students check off what progress they have made on the standard or goal. A progress bar shows students they are making progress.
>
> We designed the "SheetPusher by Alice Keeler and Heather Lyon" add-on for Google Sheets to allow you to share a copy of the graphic organizer with each student and update the goals list and push out the updates to the students.
>
> **tinyurl.com/engagementprogresstracker**

23. Noticing and Wondering

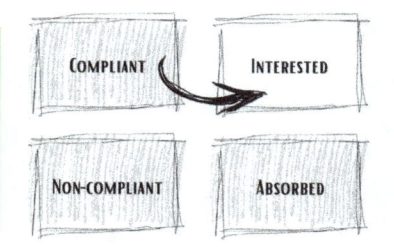

As you will recall from the beginning of the book, the 5 Es lesson plan model is structured as engage, explore, explain, extend, and evaluate. The first few minutes are our opportunity to engage students.

It's important to launch a lesson in a manner that has the students doing the thinking and the talking. Provide students with a picture and ask them what they notice and wonder. Sparking student curiosity is a great way to engage them in a lesson.

They should simply be making observations. This can be hard for some students at first because they want to skip this and go right to inferences and questions. Wonders are the questions they have about what they're seeing.

The picture that you use can be a photograph, but it can also be a graph, a three-dimensional model, a map, etc.

Try to keep a poker face as you collect student observations. In order for students to reason through an idea, they first need time to make mistakes and rethink for themselves. The key is to get the students to do the talking. As the facilitator, you can ask clarifying questions, but try to stick with neutral responses like "Great, what else do you notice?" Keep at it until students have noticed more obscure things in the image or object.

Use a Google Form or a collaborative Google Slides to allow students to share what they notice and wonder. Share the results with the students to spark a class discussion. By providing a Form with the image to start with, you can give all students an opportunity to participate.

Create a Google Form and use the IMAGE option to add a picture. Following the picture, ask, "What do you notice?" and leave room for a paragraph response.

In the same Google Form, change the question from "What do you notice" to "What do you wonder?" Students will fill out the same Google Form a second time with the updated question.

The purpose of using the Noticing and Wondering strategy in this way is to expose students to the following concepts:

1. Noticing surface initial understandings.
2. Wonders create a spark to learn more.

It also allows teachers to:

1. Create opportunities with "low floors" and "high ceilings.

TEMPLATE

Install the "Notice Wonder" add-on for Google Forms. Select SETUP to automatically create and link to a Google Slides. It is important that the first object in the Form is the image. Replace the default image. Responses to the Google Form will automatically be added to the slide after using the sidebar to send responses to Google Slides. Facilitate a conversation with the students using the generated Google Slides.

alicekeeler.com/engagementnoticewonder

24. Hyperlinking Google Slides

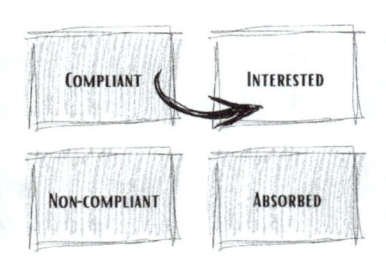

When students get to make a choice, they have a sense of a locus of control. It is not uncommon that students can go through their entire school day without being able to make any choices, even about when to go to the restroom. When students feel they get to make any decision, it can help them to feel ownership of the task—which leads to engagement.

Most of us did not have much choice when we were in school, and since so many teachers teach like they were taught, we create situations for our students where we are in charge of determining assignments. Further, when we think about choice and voice, we think about differentiated instruction (DI). DI, most often associated with Carol Ann Tomlinson, is "an approach to teaching where you actively plan for students' differences so that they can best learn." This active planning for students' differences has somehow come to mean that one teacher is supposed to create a different lesson for each child in the classroom. No elementary teacher has time to create twenty or more different lessons for each of their students for each of the subjects taught. No secondary teacher has time to create a hundred or more different lessons for each of their students. This is not realistic.

How can choice and voice happen in classrooms every day for every student? When it comes to choice, try designing a menu of different tasks that will all achieve the learning. This means focusing on what the learning is supposed to be (the standards and the skills) and then designing at least two (but it could be more) options that will achieve the learning. The students then have the all-important-to-engagement choice of what they will do in order to demonstrate their learning.

Voice is even easier. The last choice of the options can always be "Propose an option that isn't listed that would meet the outcome." Certainly, if you have students who cannot yet read, there is work that needs to be done to help students understand this model, but even then, it is possible.

When creating choices, consider students' interests. For example, do you have students who are interested in music? Is there a way for them to do the task that would incorporate that interest? Since student interests are varied, you could create a list of possible examples while also leaving opportunity for students to create options as well. You can give certain options different values so that students have to earn a total number of points to complete the tasks. These are often features of choice boards or playlists.

If creating interest is about creating tasks that students want to do AND it is easier to create tasks that students want to do by allowing them choice and voice, then the goal should be to find easy and manageable ways to create student choice and voice.

Create a choice board with Google Slides. On the first slide, create shapes or text boxes with a variety of choices. Remember, by definition the word *choices* indicates that students do not have to complete all of the options.

For each choice on the first slide, create a slide with directions. Use Ctrl+K to hyperlink the choice on the first slide to the slide of directions.

Under the FILE menu in Slides is an option to SHARE. Use PUBLISH TO THE WEB to share the link to the choice board with students.

The purpose of using the Hyperlinking Google Slides strategy in this way is to expose students to the following concepts:

1. Choice and voice lead to higher levels of engagement.
2. Not every student needs to do identical work to achieve the intended learning outcomes.

It also allows teachers to:

1. Use students' interests outside of school to create students who are interested in school.

TEMPLATE

Use the Google Slides template to create a playlist of choices.

Use the "Hyperlink Choice Board" add-on for Google Slides to speed up the process. Arrange text boxes on the first slide. Use the add-on to automatically create hyperlinks within the slide.

alicekeeler.com/engagementhyperlinks

25. Earning Badges

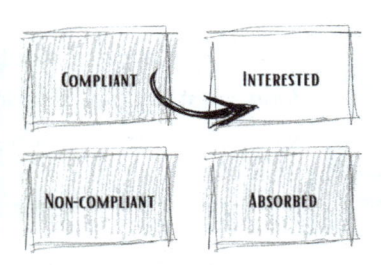

If you were ever a Boy or Girl Scout, you know a thing or two about badges, those patches that you earn by completing a series of tasks to demonstrate your proficiency in a skill. No scout is required to earn all badges, nor are they all required to earn the same badges—there are options for identifying the skills you have mastered.

This same idea can be applied to classrooms. The key to doing it successfully is to (a) be willing to generate multiple pathways for the students to demonstrate success, including, but not limited to, students having the chance to work collaboratively and/or independently and (b) be open to the possibility that your first attempt at this will ultimately need revision. The goal is to get started so you can revise later—not to delay starting until it is perfect. So, if you're willing to take the risk, you'll do the following:

- Clearly identify the intended learning.
- Determine what the students will need to do in order to demonstrate they have achieved the intended learning.
- Create tiers of tasks—some that are required and some that are optional—that students will do to demonstrate their learning.

Since this will be just as new for the students as it is for you, it will be important to frontload the learning with clear directions and expectations. Then, because the learning was planned in advance behind the scenes, you will be available to the students during the learning work time to assist them when and if they need it. You will also be able to monitor the learning in case there is instruction that you didn't plan for but might be needed.

Eventually, and this might take quite a bit of time, you could have a classroom where students are working on different badges because their learning is determined by their interest in different topics. As well, you can invite the students at the end of the experience to offer suggestions for changes to the process.

Imagine, for example, that you created a unit on biomes and students might all need to earn at least three of six possible badges related to the unit. Since the work is self-paced, you might have a couple students working together on one badge, while you're doing a conference with students working on different badges but all in need of support with a skill like citations, and the rest of the class is working independently on their learning. The ways this could look in your classroom are truly endless.

Generally, there are three reasons to have badges:

- For fun
- To show mastery
- To challenge students to go further

Before creating a badging system, start small. Consider badges students can earn over a week or over a unit.

Creating badges is the first hurdle; tracking the earning of badges will be the second.

One way to design badges is in Google Drawings. Go to drawings.google.com and use the FILE menu to select PAGE SETUP to customize the size. Make the canvas square. We suggest 5 inches by 5 inches.

When creating badges, make a perfect circle or a perfect square. Hold down the SHIFT key when creating shapes to accomplish this. Near the fill color in the toolbar is the LINE-WEIGHT option. Make the border of your shape much thicker to give it the appearance of a badge.

After creating your badges, use the FILE menu in Google Drawings to DOWNLOAD AS A PNG. This allows you to add the badge to Google Docs, Slides, or Sites. You can also add this PNG image into cells in Google Sheets by using the INSERT menu and selecting INSERT IMAGE IN CELL.

Consider using Google Sheets to create a list of the tasks that earn students a badge. Check off the tasks with checkboxes in the spreadsheet.

Once a student has accomplished the criteria for earning a badge, you will need a system to award the badge. Commonly, distributing the badges is the hardest part, but there are a plethora of ways to distribute the badge image to students. Using the "Certify'em" add-on for Google Forms can allow you to have students fill out a Form for the badge. The digital image can then be automatically sent to them on a certificate. Another method is to have one Google Slides per student. Add each badge image to a master Google Slide to easily copy and paste the slide to individual students.

TEMPLATE

Use Alice Keeler's Badge Game template to create a level-up choice board in Google Sheets. The template allows you to assign badges to quests. These badges are displayed when the quest is checked off. As the student completes quests, they level up. Use the badge game as a single assignment with a criteria to reach a certain level before adding the assignment to the gradebook.

tinyurl.com/engagementbadgegame

The purpose of using the Earning Badges strategy in this way is to expose students to the following concepts:

1. Learning doesn't have to be linear.
2. Not every student needs to do identical work to achieve the intended learning outcomes.

It also allows teachers to:

1. Use extrinsic motivators like earning a badge to help students find interest and see a record of what they have learned (and earned).

26. Checking for Feedback

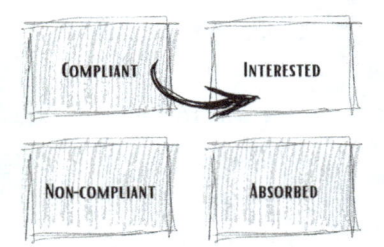

One of the challenges of giving feedback is that students often don't look at it. This is because we too often give grades at the same time the students get the feedback—meaning there is nothing that the student can do with the feedback. Feedback that comes as the last part in an assignment is "autopsy feedback." It's only value is for future assignments, not to improve what was already graded. There is no need to give feedback at that point; the feedback should have been given before the grade so the student had the chance to use it.

In fact, when feedback is given to students at the same time grades are provided, students often disregard the feedback and go straight to the grades. The teacher's intention was to help the student in the future, but the student won't really pay attention to the feedback and won't use it in the future. Accordingly, the teacher gets frustrated and feels like they've wasted their time.

The problem isn't that the students aren't interested in feedback—it's that the timing of the feedback is all wrong. Consider providing feedback before grades. Once students are given the feedback, they can respond to the feedback and even make changes to revise their work. This deepens the original assignment into a more formative learning opportunity. In other words, the assignment goes from being an autopsy (where no changes can be made) to a physical (where there is still the opportunity to grow).

When a student submits an assignment, provide feedback via one or more comments. The last comment Heather likes to make when using this approach is a question: "Based on the feedback I gave you and the rubric for this assignment, what grade do you think this assignment earned and why?" This allows Heather to see how well the students understood both the feedback and the rubric. This is especially important if the format of the assignment and/or the rubric is something the students will repeatedly see.

In fact, many times, students will comment on future assignments with something like "Based on the feedback from my last reflection, I made sure to attend to _____ in this reflection."

Use the Ctrl+Alt+M keyboard shortcut to insert comments.

You may want to add the student's name to several of the comments for more personalized feedback. Ctrl+Enter saves the comment to save you additional time when leaving feedback.

Return work to the students with the directive to click on the COMMENT icon in the upper right of the Google Doc. This will allow students to not only quickly see the feedback comments that were left but to jump down to the relevant spot in the document, where they can update their work.

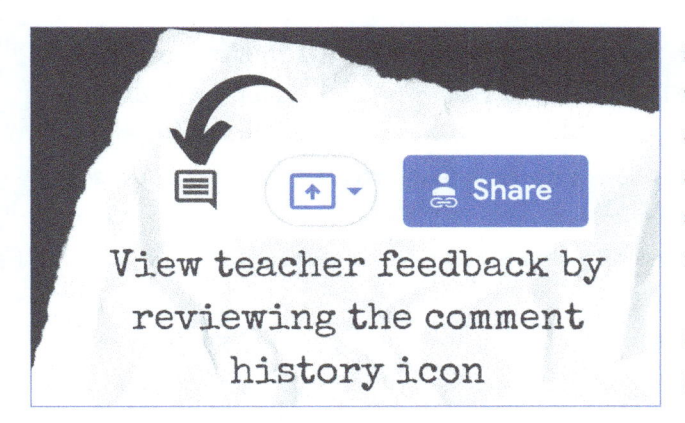

View teacher feedback by reviewing the comment history icon

Students can resubmit their work after responding to the feedback. This provides the opportunity to assess their growth. If they respond to the feedback adequately, consider giving them full credit. This shows you are there to HELP them rather than just mark down points.

It is much more engaging knowing you are going to learn and improve rather than be evaluated.

The purpose of using the Checking for Feedback strategy in this way is to expose students to the following concepts:

1. Learning is a process, not an event.
2. When students and teachers interact prior to grading, the learning process is prioritized.
3. Revisions lead to improvements.
4. Purposeful collaboration can positively impact learning and results.

TEMPLATE

When assigning students individual Google Docs, make them a copy of the template. This will remind them to check the COMMENTS icon at the top of the Google Doc to see what feedback you have left them recently.

tinyurl.com/engagementfeedbackcomments

27. Connecting with Authentic Audiences

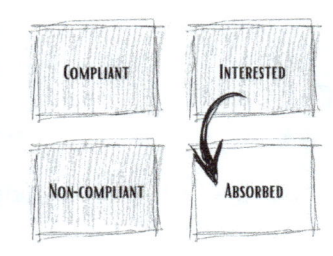

If children put a lot of work into an essay or project or get a good grade on one, they may run home to tell their parents about what they've done. However, generally, doing work just for the purpose of handing it in for a grade is not very engaging. And even if the learning is meant to be persuasive or informational, the only person likely to look at the final product is the teacher, because the product is artificial. Artificial work rarely generates engagement.

It is not uncommon for students to write a letter to the principal to try to get them to give more recess time or allow use of cell phones in the cafeteria, etc. This is certainly better than writing for the teacher exclusively. Nevertheless, if you are working on learning something in science, social studies, art, or physical education, it might make sense to include professional scientists, historians, artists, or athletes as possible audience members. Making connections to people outside of the walls of the school ups the ante for putting true effort into a task. It's even better if there is the possibility that the person will respond.

Imagine if students wrote to authors of books they are reading rather than writing a book summary or review exclusively for a grade from a teacher? What if, while studying space, students used social media to contact to someone at NASA, the International Space Station, or Neil DeGrasse Tyson? When studying your country's involvement in conflicts, ask a veteran to come in to speak, then invite that person back to listen to the students share what they have learned and participate in a discussion with them.

An authentic audience increases the value of the assignment. Students are not simply turning something in to their teacher, they are creating something of value for an outside audience.

Digital documents are an excellent way to help students create work for an authentic audience, and the collaborative nature of Google Apps allows for peer and teacher feedback to ensure the words are just right before sending.

Students can write letters to politicians in a Google Doc. The document can be printed and mailed or sent using the EMAIL option in the Google Docs FILE menu. This will attach the letter as a PDF to send in an email.

Students wanting to make a change in their community will need to present their ideas. Creating a persuasive presentation in Google Slides with carefully chosen images and text will help them more effectively deliver their message to an authentic audience.

When a live presentation is not possible, consider having students organize their work onto a Google Sites web page. This allows for them to connect with a large community instead of just one community member. Google Sites are collaborative, thus allowing multiple students to work together to research and communicate the problem and the suggested solution. Unlike a Google Doc, Sites are multimedia, allowing for video and audio to be included to create a bigger impact.

Have students go to sites.google.com to create a new Google Site for the project. Only one site per group is needed. If all students in the class are tackling the same project, they can work on the same Google Site together, each making their arguments on different pages of the site. This makes it easier for community members to review the different perspectives. With parent/guardian permission, make the website visible outside of the school domain and share it on social media where appropriate.

> **SAMPLE**
> Provide students with tips on how to utilize a Google Site as a website to share their project.
>
> alicekeeler.com/engagingauthenticaudience

The purpose of using the Connecting with Authentic Audiences strategy in this way is to expose students to the following concepts:

1. Learning is not confined to a classroom or even to school.
2. Audience matters.
3. Students are people who have something to say, no matter how old they are.
4. Teachers are not the only people interested in what students have to say.

28. Hosting Virtual Parent Meetings

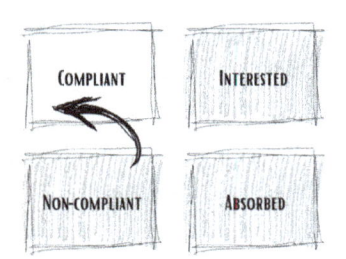

When schools see families as partners, engagement from students increases. Sometimes, that simply translates to higher levels of compliance (like students being more likely to do their homework). Other times, partnerships between school and home yield even greater returns by fostering a supportive learning environment that promotes collaboration, communication, and shared responsibility for the student's success.

Though there are barriers that can get in the way of forming partnerships, the inability to meet should not be one of them. If we learned anything from the pandemic, it's that meeting with people virtually is possible. While there are times when in-person meetings are necessary, quite honestly, working families or families who have limited transportation options prefer to meet virtually.

Chris Hayhurst wrote about this in his EdTech article "More of Today's Parent-Teacher Meetings are Happening Virtually," from October 6, 2022:

> [Lewisville ISD] leaders thought they would only need to offer remote meetings temporarily, but soon realized many parents preferred the option. "Rather than having to get time off from work and schedule their day around coming in to a meeting, now they can connect with us from anywhere," he says.

For parents, these virtual conferences can take place on whatever devices they happen to have. Some use their own smartphones or laptops, while others turn to the school-issued tablets the district deploys to students through its one-to-one program.

The preference for virtual meetings was not isolated to Lewisville. The International Society for Technology in Education (ISTE) saw the same trends across the country, notes Hayhurst.

> "Attendance at parent-teacher conferences skyrocketed during the pandemic," says ISTE Chief Learning Officer Joseph South. "It wasn't because parents suddenly became interested in the success of their children; it was because suddenly those conferences were a lot more accessible to parents with obligations that weren't flexible."

Simply put, working together with guardians can help the school gain insights that can help keep students engaged. Technology allows us to open up additional opportunities to collaborate and communicate with guardians, fostering a strong partnership that supports student learning and growth.

Time is limited for everyone. Opening up collaboration with guardians to virtual options allows for more guardian participation.

Google Meet is a virtual meeting platform, and a Meet link can be shared with a parent.

Create a Google Calendar event with a Google Meet integrated. In the description of the Google Calendar event, create an agenda or talking points to communicate with the guardian.

In the Google Calendar event, use the PAPER CLIP icon to add student work samples for the guardian to review prior to the meeting.

To allow guardians to find times that work for their schedules, take advantage of the APPOINTMENT SLOTS option in Google for Education Calendar events. This allows the teacher to block off times that they are available to meet with guardians. Share the calendar link to allow guardians to choose a slot and easily access the Google Meet.

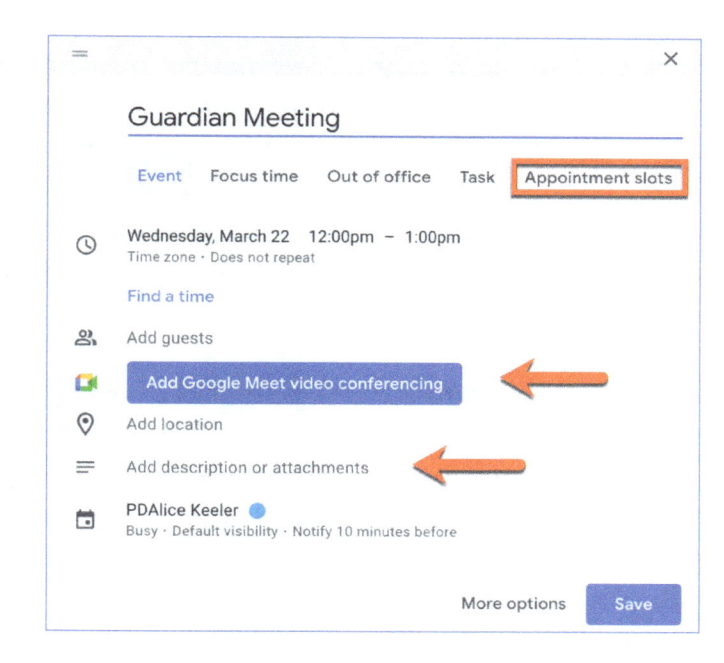

The purpose of using the Hosting Virtual Parent Meetings strategy in this way is to expose students to the following concepts:

1. Families and schools are working together to support the student's learning and growth.

It also allows teachers to:

1. Ensure that there is open communication between the family and the school, helping both parties understand the student's needs and how best to support them.
2. Ensure that expectations, learning strategies, and support are consistent between home and school to help students stay on track.

> **RESOURCE**
>
> Use the "CalAdd" add-on for Google Sheets to batch create Google Calendar events to meet with guardians.

29. Forming Groups

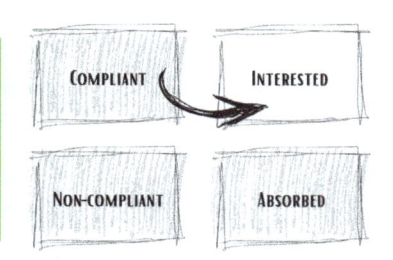

Group work, when done purposefully, can lead to high levels of engagement. Be careful, however, because not all group work is created equally.

We have all been there: Assigned to work in a group and yet the task we were doing was something we could have actually done more easily by ourselves. We have also been assigned group work that was really just busywork. Neither of these scenarios captures the true power or intended purpose of collaboration.

In fact, the purpose of group work should always be to achieve an outcome that is not possible without working together. Asking students to do something collaboratively that they could achieve independently may actually decrease engagement.

There is a long list of reasons why group work can be highly engaging, including, but not limited to social interaction, hands-on/active learning, navigating diverse perspectives, etc. Assuming the group work is something that requires a group, it truly can be highly engaging. When designed and implemented effectively, it not only promotes collaboration and communication but also fosters a deeper understanding of the material being taught.

Group work is improved by creating accountability, so that the teacher knows who did what in order to reduce the "work grabber" or the "work avoider" effect. That doesn't mean students are parallel playing (like toddlers in a sandbox making separate castles); they should be interacting—potentially with unique roles and responsibilities to achieve a shared outcome.

Students need to be taught how to effectively work in groups, and Google Docs or Sheets can be an excellent tool to help provide structure for successful group work.

Set clear objectives in the Google Doc. Define the learning goals for each group task and ensure that they align with your curriculum and overall objectives for the lesson. This will give students a clear sense of purpose and help them stay focused on the task at hand.

Design meaningful tasks that require critical thinking, problem-solving, and creativity, rather than simple tasks that can be completed individually. Meaningful tasks will encourage collaboration and keep students engaged.

Assign specific roles to each group member, such as facilitator, recorder, or presenter. This will help ensure that each student has a clear responsibility and contributes to the group's success. Have students create a rubric for their job to create a "contract" to clearly outline what they are going to be responsible for.

In the Google Doc or Sheet, set expectations for group behavior, such as listening to others, taking turns speaking, and staying on task. Make sure students understand these rules and the importance of following them.

Provide structure by breaking tasks into smaller, manageable steps and provide clear instructions for each step. This will help students stay organized and focused, and ensure that they understand what is expected of them. Add dropdowns to the Google Doc or Sheets to allow students to indicate where they are for each task.

Create groups with mixed abilities and interests in mind. This diversity will encourage students to learn from one another and expose them to new perspectives and ideas.

Regularly check in with each group to ensure that they are on track and working effectively. Provide guidance and support as needed, and be prepared to adjust the task or group dynamics if necessary. Using Google Docs, the teacher can review group progress before the due date.

Encourage reflection by having students discuss what worked well, what challenges they faced, and what they learned. This reflection can help students develop metacognitive skills and improve their performance in future group work.

Evaluate both the group's overall performance and each student's individual contribution to the group. Provide feedback on how well students met the learning objectives, collaborated with their peers, and fulfilled their assigned roles.

The purpose of using the Forming Groups strategy in this way is to expose students to the following concepts:

1. Collective intelligence leads to better outcomes than what any single person is able to do independently.
2. Purposeful collaboration can positively impact learning and results.

> **TEMPLATE**
>
> The Group Work template helps students structure group responsibilities and tasks. Group members can take ownership of project elements and use the dropdown lists to indicate their status.
>
> **tinyurl.com/engagementgroupwork**

30. Personalizing with Names

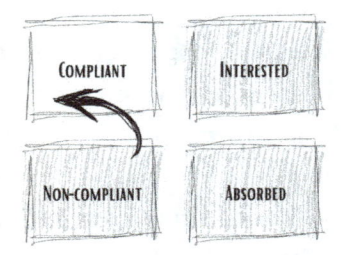

Relationships are a key aspect of engagement. In fact, relationships can be the difference between whether a student is non-compliant or at a higher level of engagement. Students are more engaged when they feel the teacher cares about them.

One way to make connections with students is to type or say their name as often as possible. When providing feedback, instead of "Good job," use "Good job, Hedreich." Both verbal and written feedback have more power when the student hears or sees their name.

Feedback can come in many forms. In addition to leaving text feedback, consider leaving audio or video feedback. Sign up at mote.com to be able to leave students audio notes. Start your audio comment with their name. When people hear their name, they lean in. Try to include the student's name in the audio recording multiple times, if possible.

If you are going to review student work, consider screen recording while you do it. This makes it easy to provide a visual along with audio of your feedback. Screencastify is a Chrome extension that makes it easy to record your screen and provide the video to the student. During the recording, use the students name: "Vernon, I really like how you have written the first sentence of your essay. But, Vernon, you need to check for commas. Vernon, you have great things you are listing, but you're not using enough commas." After creating the screen recording, you can copy the link to the video to your clipboard with Screencastify, making it easy to paste the link where you would normally leave text feedback.

In addition, using a student's name has the psychological effect of indicating to the student that you care about them. Students are going to work harder in class when they feel that the teacher cares about them as a person.

Feedback where you type a student's name can be left in comments in a Google Doc, private comments in Google Classroom, or in an email. Even when copying and pasting feedback comments, consider editing the pasted comment to include the student's name.

To simplify the process of customizing feedback comments, consider utilizing the concatenate function in Google Sheets. This function enables you to "smash together" a feedback comment and the student's name, making it more personalized.

One way to concatenate student names with feedback text is to use the ampersand symbol (&). Any feedback text will need to be between "double quotes."

In one column of a spreadsheet, paste the students' names. In the next column, use cell referencing to write a comment that concatenates with the student's name.

For example, if in A2 you have the student's name, then in B2 you would start with an equals sign as follows:

> =A2&", you have done a great job with your topic sentence. " &A2& ", next time you will want to develop your full introduction paragraph."

Press Enter and then go back and click on the cell with the feedback. Use Ctrl+C to copy the feedback comment. Use Ctrl+Shift+V to paste the comment where you desire to leave feedback to the student.

If you want to leave the same comment to multiple students, yet personalize it, take advantage of the fill-down square. When you click on the cell with personalized feedback, take notice of the small square in the bottom right of the cell. This is the fill-down square. Drag this square down to copy the formula for each of the other students.

This will help you to quickly create personalized feedback comments. Copy and paste these comments when needed.

The purpose of using the Personalizing with Names strategy in this way is to expose students to the following concepts:

1. Hearing your own name is a form of positive reinforcement.

It also allows teachers to:

1. Create a sense of relationship between the student and the teacher.
2. Maximize the likelihood that all students will be able to participate in the learning.

TEMPLATE

In this template you can paste your class roster into column A. Write or copy a feedback comment in column B. A personalized comment will automatically be created in column C that you can copy and paste to students.

tinyurl.com/engagementname

31. Rethinking Learning Loss

Have you ever looked at a clock and realized you were late to something? Depending on how late you were, you might have even wondered if it was worth going at all. Unfortunately, feeling like you're behind is often demotivating.

The term *learning loss* was used during the pandemic and afterward. It suggests students did not learn as much as they were supposed to during the pandemic. While that might be true, the reality is that "learning loss" sounds negative—it implies that students have lost or regressed in their learning, which can be discouraging for both students and educators. As well, the term suggests that students are falling behind, which can create a sense of defeatism and lower expectations for student success. The implication of learning loss is that learning has been lost forever. But learning is a dynamic and ongoing process that can be regained with appropriate support and interventions, and that should be acknowledged.

Instead, terms like *unfinished learning* or *learning recovery* reflect a more positive and proactive approach to supporting students' academic growth and development.

With or without a pandemic, some students will still experience unfinished learning. Why? Because people are not widgets, and everyone learns at a different pace. What's more, insufficient prior knowledge decreases student engagement because when people lack skill, their desire to participate in the task (will) can also be low.

If the goal is to engage students in learning they may have missed or misunderstood, then it's important we (a) frame it so they remain motivated and (b) use strategies to help them see their progress. Google Gemini is an artificial intelligence (AI) technology that can be used in the classroom to enhance student learning. AI refers to the ability of machines to perform tasks that would typically require human intelligence, such as natural language processing and decision-making. Including AI technology like Google Gemini in the classroom can provide teachers with powerful tools to personalize learning, adapt assessments, and provide students with feedback and support in real time. This can lead to improved student outcomes and more engaged and motivated learners. Additionally, AI technology can free up teacher time, allowing them to focus on other aspects of teaching while still providing students with individualized attention and support.

To ensure that students can meet grade-level standards, it's important to acknowledge that there may be gaps in their knowledge or skills. Allowing students to use Google Gemini, helps them access the information they need to address the standards at high levels. This can provide students with personalized support and guidance, helping them to fill in any gaps and improve their overall understanding of the material.

Using an AI chatbot requires refining the questions you ask. Start by asking Gemini for prerequisite skills needed for a student to be able to learn the standard. If the results are not what you were looking for, prompt Gemini to update the response to include, exclude, or consider a topic.

> **TEMPLATE**
>
> This infographic describes how to use an AI chatbot to provide scaffolding for a student who has a gap in their knowledge needed for a particular lesson.
>
> **tinyurl.com/Engagement-AI**

Continue having a conversation with Gemini to elicit tutorials, relatable examples for students, or scaffolding to help students be able to participate in the grade-level lesson.

The purpose of using the Rethinking Learning Loss strategy in this way is to expose students to the following concepts:

1. Keep motivation high.
2. Ensure learning is maintained.
3. Focus limited resources on high priority learning.

32. Rebranding with Gamification

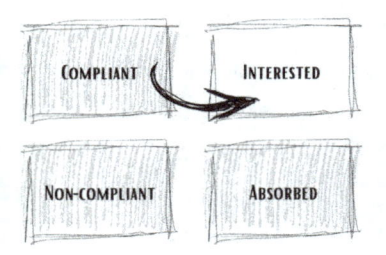

Gamification is engaging because it transforms learning into a fun and interactive experience that can motivate and empower students. It incorporates game design elements such as collaboration, exploration, and feedback, which can enhance the learning experience and promote student success.

Gamification can promote collaboration and teamwork by creating opportunities for students to work together toward a common goal. By encouraging students to share knowledge and resources, gamification can foster a supportive learning environment that encourages students to help each other and learn from one another.

Gamification can also promote exploration and discovery by providing students with opportunities to explore new topics and learn through trial and error. By incorporating game-like challenges, puzzles, and simulations, students can engage in hands-on learning experiences that allow them to experiment with new ideas and approaches.

Additionally, gamification can provide immediate feedback, progress tracking, and personalized learning experiences. By incorporating feedback loops and adaptive learning technologies, students can receive real-time feedback on their performance and adjust their learning strategies accordingly.

Overall, gamification can make learning more engaging, interactive, and enjoyable by incorporating game-design elements that promote collaboration, exploration, feedback, and personalization. By emphasizing these elements, teachers can create a motivating and stimulating learning environment that can help students develop new skills and achieve academic success.

Google Slides shines as a game board template for displaying questions. Use it to re-create popular games as review games.

Take advantage of the hyperlinking possibilities to allow students to select a question. Select an object on the slides and use Ctrl+K to create the hyperlink to another slide or resource.

Games with hyperlink elements need to be shared in presentation mode. Oftentimes, games are played with the whole class, and the teacher is able to simply click the SLIDESHOW button to facilitate the game.

When sharing with students, use the FILE MENU and the SHARE option. Select PUBLISH to the web. The link provides the game in presentation mode.

To create a Jeopardy!-style game, try using the "Hyperlink Slides Choice Board" add-on for Google Slides. Add a shape for each dollar amount. Use the add-on to automatically create linked slides for each question.

TEMPLATE

Use the template to create a Pictionary-style game from the unit vocabulary words in a Google Doc. Create a copy of the Pictionary template and paste the link to the Slides into the sidebar of the "Doc to Slides" add-on for Google Docs. This will automatically create a Frayer model for each vocabulary word within the Google Slides.

After students have created the Frayer slides, use the "Randomize Slides" add-on to shuffle the words. Divide the students up into teams. The artist at the board will be able to see a computer screen with the vocabulary word in presentation mode. The screen should only be visible to the artist. Advance to the next slide for the next word for the next artist.

tinyurl.com/engagementpictionary

Use the Class Baseball template for a *Jeopardy!*-style review game with an opportunity for students to get out of their seats.

tinyurl.com/engagementclassbaseball

The purpose of using the Rebranding with Gamification strategy in this way is to expose students to the following concepts:

1. Learning can be more enjoyable and memorable (which can increase students' engagement and retention of the material).

It also allows teachers to:

1. Organize learning content into levels of increasing complexity or difficulty.
2. Provide timely feedback and encouragement to students to celebrate their successes and guide them through challenges.

33. Creating with Pixel Art

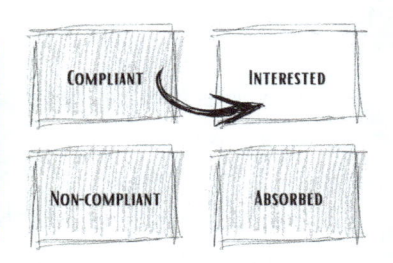

Getting to the interested level on the Engagement Matrix does not necessarily require challenge—it requires giving students a task they want to do and an extrinsic consequence that matters to them. In other words, we need to hook them. Once we get them hooked, we unlock more avenues to extend engagement.

Writing answers down on a line in any format is not particularly exciting. To engage learners, we want to offer them choice and voice in the task they are doing. This means that their final product does not necessarily match their neighbor's assignment.

Look for ways to start an assignment with something creative for students to do that can be tied into the learning objective. Students then build off of their creations.

Students from pre-K to high school enjoy pixel art activities where they get to design an image in small squares.

Google Sheets allows you to utilize conditional formatting so that when a value is entered into a cell, it is color coded. Setting the conditional formatting font and fill color to be the same allows for a paint by number experience within the spreadsheet.

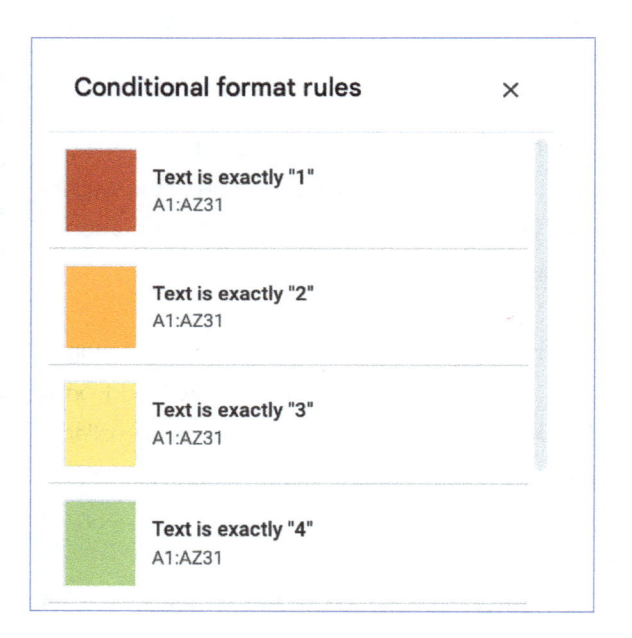

Begin a lesson by inviting students to craft an image of their choice using a Pixel Art template. Once they have completed their distinctive designs, these images will serve as the launching pad for the assignment at hand. No matter the topic, students can start by visualizing with a creative picture. Give the

TEMPLATE

The Google Sheets Pixel Art template is set up to allow you to easily assign a copy to each student. Ask students to type single-digit numbers into the spreadsheet to create their image.

tinyurl.com/engagementpixelart

students a challenge related to the topic and see how they accomplish it using pixelated images in a spreadsheet.

The purpose of using the Creating with Pixel Art strategy in this way is to expose students to the following concepts:

1. Creativity leads to investment in work.

It also allows teachers to:

1. Spark engagement through choice and voice.
2. Create opportunities with "low floors" and "high ceilings."

34. Celebrating Success through Calls Home

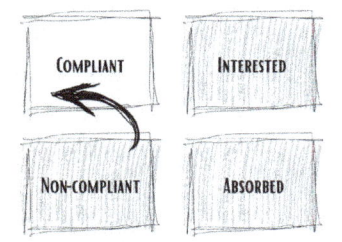

In 2004, Marcial Losada and Emily Heaphy's study "The Role of Positivity and Connectivity in the Performance of Business Teams: A Nonlinear Dynamics Model" was published in the journal *American Behavioral Scientist*.[2] While their research was unrelated to schools, they found the ideal praise-to-criticism ratio for teams is 5:1. Meaning, for every negative comment you make, you need to share five positive comments as well. What's more, low-functioning business teams actually shared more negative feedback than positive, or three times as many negative comments for each positive comment.

Schools have teams too. In fact, the school teams with families to ensure success for students. Unfortunately, in schools, the adage "No news is good news" tends to be the norm. As such, schools will communicate neutral information about all kids regularly (e.g., generic newsletters) but personalized information is commonly limited to report cards and instances of individual student misbehavior. If we really want to make families our partners, then we need to amp up our positive interactions.

Making positive phone calls home is a highly effective strategy to increase student engagement. By regularly communicating with parents and guardians about their child's achievements, progress, and positive behaviors, we create supportive learning environments that benefit the student, family, and teacher.

---

2   Marcial Losada and Emily Heaphy, "The Role of Positivity and Connectivity in the Performance of Business Teams: A Nonlinear Dynamics Model," *American Behavioral Scientist* 47, no. 6 (2004): 740–65.

Google Sheets is an excellent tool for keeping track of parent/guardian contacts. Create columns for the following items:

- Date of contact
- Student name
- Who was contacted
- Reason for the contact
- Notes from the call

It is important to consistently record the student's name in the spreadsheet. In a different sheet, create a list of student names. If any students share the same name, be sure to include an indicator such as middle initial or student ID number to make each name in the list unique.

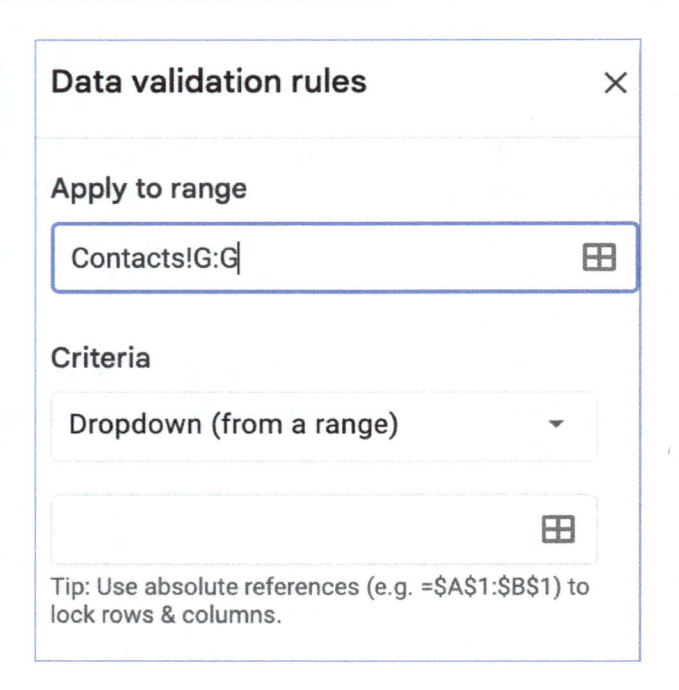

Use data validation rules in Google Sheets to create a dropdown from a range. Instead of typing a student's name, select the student name or ID number from a dropdown list.

Use the "toTabs" add-on for Google Sheets to automatically separate logs per student into individual tabs. This makes it easy to know how often a student's parent/guardian has been contacted.

Using the Contact Log template, send emails to guardians at the same time you document the contact. Use the ADD-ON menu to send emails.

The purpose of using the Celebrating Success through Calls Home strategy in this way is to expose students to the following concepts:

1. Their family and the school are on the same team and the same page, acknowledging and sharing efforts and achievements.

It also allows teachers to:

1. Recognize and celebrate successes with parents, which can significantly improve student self-esteem and confidence.

TEMPLATE

Use this Contact Log template to keep a record of any guardian contacts that are made. The included pivot table displays how many times each student's guardians were contacted. The SEND EMAIL menu at the top allows you to contact guardians directly from the template.

tinyurl.com/engagementcontactlog

2. Create trusting relationships with parents so they will be more likely to discuss concerns and seek guidance from teachers, ultimately contributing to increased student engagement

35. Building Small Wins

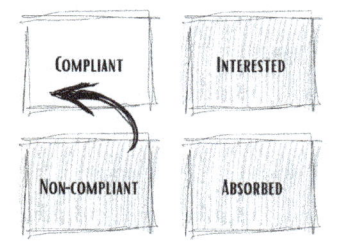

Heather was a nonrunner. In fact, when she was in school, she faked an asthma attack rather than run one mile for the Presidential Physical Fitness Test. It's not that she couldn't run, what she lacked was experience and skill running smaller distances to build up to the mile—and a lack of will to run in the first place.

In her late thirties, Heather found some will to run and learned about the Couch to 5K app, which she downloaded to her phone. She learned that by using smaller intervals, she could become a runner. The app didn't have her run a 5K on the first day; instead, the goal of the first week of running was to run eight intervals of sixty seconds sandwiched between intervals of ninety seconds of walking. This occurred three times in the first week. Each week, there was a new interval that increased the distance and amount of time running and decreased the distance and amount of time walking. Through these little goals with little increases to build her running skills, Heather was ultimately able to run a 5K. However, if you had asked Heather to run a 5K on day one, she would have again opted out.

Why does a student choose not to do an assignment? While there is no simple answer for this, one culprit may be a lack of confidence. If they do not do the task, they won't be seen as dumb—just as not having completed it.

Put differently, when someone has low self-efficacy, they are more likely to do nothing, because they feel like even if they do try, they'll be unsuccessful. They will avoid the task until it never gets done. So, just like Heather's app, we need to give students smaller, scaffolded intervals so they know they are making progress and so they are not asked to do something beyond their ability level. How? Provide several small things students can do to help them avoid doing nothing.

Many students need help just getting started.

Use Google Sheets to create a checklist for students to help them log small wins to build up to larger successes. This is not a choice board but rather a list of things the student can do ordered from easy wins to tougher challenges.

Add checkboxes to Google Sheets under the INSERT menu. The sparkline function can be used to a cell in Google Sheets to show a progress bar for the student checking off the tasks. A BAR-CHART sparkline in Google Sheets compares the number of tasks completed to the total number of tasks. The bar in the cell acts as a progress bar.

To use this function, try something like the following:

=sparkline(D2,{"charttype","bar";"max",B2})

The purpose of using the Building Small Wins strategy in this way is to expose students to the following concepts:

1. The journey of a thousand miles starts with one step.
2. There is always something, however small, that students are capable of doing.
3. Doing manageable tasks builds both confidence and capability.

> **TEMPLATE**
> This spreadsheet template includes a progress bar that increases the bar length as the student checks off tasks toward a goal.
>
> **tinyurl.com/engagementsmallsteps**

36. Aiming for Mastery

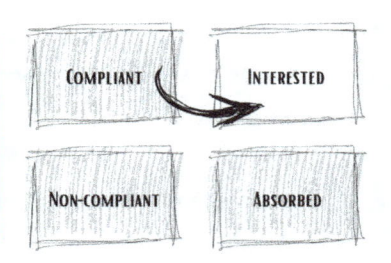

Dr. Corrie Giles, Heather's advisor in her doctoral program, once said, "If time is the constant, learning is the variable; said the other way, if learning is the constant, time is the variable."

At its heart, mastery learning is an approach that requires students to redo their work until they reach a minimum level of mastery (say 80 percent accuracy). The key to a mastery-based classroom is that students keep going until they demonstrate an acceptable level of competence with each key standard. The upside to this approach is learning becomes the constant. If the purpose of school is learning, there are few better ways to achieve this end than mastery learning.

Unfortunately—and this is the reality that is our educational system—mastery learning can be difficult because grades are due or students put off doing the work or it's time consuming to go back and review student work again. Giving a student a low score and moving on does not embrace the mastery learning concept.

Getting students to initially understand and appreciate mastery learning can be a tough sell at first, especially when many students' experiences in school are of the one-and-done, get-it-right-the-first-time variety. Yet, when teachers start with creating a classroom culture that focuses on learning and making a safe place to try—and, possibly initially fail—students come to appreciate the chance to continue to revise and show what they have come to know.

Mastery can be demonstrated in many ways, not just through a multiple-choice test. However, multiple choice can be part of the evidence toward mastery of a topic.

Create a Google Form with a dropdown for each of the key standards that students must show mastery on.

Since all students will not all demonstrate mastery on a key standard at the same time, use the Google Form to allow each student to report their success. On the RESPONSES tab, use the three-dots menu to select GET EMAIL NOTIFICATIONS FOR NEW RESPONSES. In the connected spreadsheet, add additional columns to indicate if the student indeed showed mastery and note what they did well and what they still need to demonstrate.

Pivot tables in Google Sheets are intended to summarize data. Use the PIVOT TABLE feature under the INSERT menu on the connected Google Sheet. Filter for each student's email address. Indicate rows for each standard and columns for Yes/Not Yet in the pivot table. Use this to keep track of whether each student has submitted sufficient evidence toward mastery of each key standard.

The purpose of using the Aiming for Mastery strategy in this way is to expose students to the following concepts:

1. Feeling more in control of their learning and reducing the anxiety or pressure associated with keeping up with their peers.
2. Receiving regular feedback and assessments builds understanding of their strengths and weaknesses.

> **TEMPLATE**
>
> This Form template, which collects information that can be linked to Google Sheets, is an easy way for teachers to keep track of which students have mastered which standards as well as the students' reflections on their progress.
>
> **tinyurl.com/engagementmasteryform**

It also allows teachers to:

1. Personalize pacing, to honor the fact that every student learns differently, so students are able to progress at their own pace.
2. Promote a growth mindset, as students learn that they can improve their skills and achieve mastery with persistence and practice.
3. Promote a more inclusive learning environment where all students can succeed and eliminate learning gaps.

37. Assessing the Standards

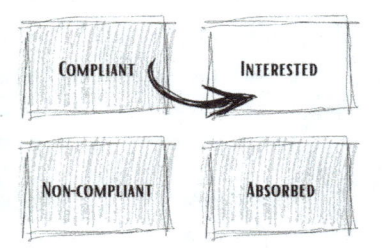

In a traditional classroom setting, students complete the assigned assignments and the average of the points earned on the assignments determine the final grade in the course. However, neither students nor the way to demonstrate knowledge of the standards are monoliths.

Students are different people with different interests, talents, and paces for learning. Standards simply state the destination of the learning, but not how to get there. Pacing guides and a "test on Friday" assume everyone learns the same way at the same time. Some students don't learn slower than others due to a lack of intelligence—just the opposite: Taking time to think and process can help students learn material better.

When the model in a classroom is solely built around completing assignments and moving on to the next task rather than identifying the learning standards (destination) and multiple ways to demonstrate achievement, students may be less engaged and motivated in their learning. This is because the emphasis is on the end result rather than the learning process. Students simply aim to earn a score and move on to the next assignment, rather than focusing on truly understanding the material and mastering the topic.

In contrast, a multiple-pathway model allows students to choose a path that allows them to tap into their preferences and still achieve the learning. This offers students a deeper understanding of the material tested. As a result, students may be more engaged and invested in their learning, as they feel a sense of accomplishment and mastery when they successfully demonstrate their knowledge.

Redesigning the structure of a class from a traditional do-the-task model to a standards-based pathway system shifts the outcomes and the engagement level.

Instead of setting up your Google Classroom or learning management system of choice as a collection of assignments, consider organizing by key standards.

Create one topic per key standard. For the assignment under the topic, create an assignment for students to submit their evidence of mastery of the key standard. Try to avoid mentioning the product the students will produce in the rubric of the Google Classroom assignment. For instance, instead of "Create a poster" you could use, "Create a project that shows your application of the key standard."

Google Classroom allows students to submit any file type to an assignment. They can submit a video, Google Doc, audio recording, or other media type.

Students can use Private Comments in Google Classroom to reflect on their submission and to explain what they learned and why the submission demonstrates the key standard.

The purpose of using the Assessing the Standards strategy in this way is to expose students to the following concepts:

1. Choice fuels engagement.
2. There are multiple methods to demonstrate learning of the standards.
3. Learning is deepened when there are options in how to learn.

> **TEMPLATE**
>
> Use the "GC Rubric" add-on for Google Sheets to create rubrics for each standard. Organize each rubric in a folder in Google Drive. Choose IMPORT FROM SHEETS for the rubric in a Google Classroom assignment.

38. Rethinking Grading

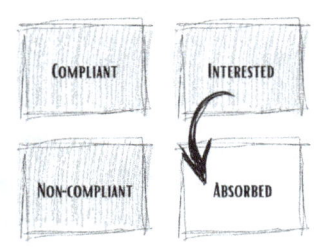

When we give students grades in the absence of or in the place of feedback, we are teaching them that the grade matters and that the learning is, at best, secondary. Stop grading and ask students, "Where were you successful here?"

While grades have traditionally been a cornerstone of the educational system, they may not be the most effective way to engage students in learning. Instead, providing meaningful feedback is more engaging and conducive to fostering deeper understanding and long-term retention of knowledge.

Surprisingly to some, grading has limitations that can affect the learning process in several ways. Grades often put more emphasis on the outcome of learning than the learning process itself, which can result in a focus on performance rather than growth. This approach can limit the scope of what students learn, and they may miss out on the benefits of a broader understanding of the subject. Additionally, extrinsic motivation, such as the pursuit of grades, can undermine intrinsic motivation, which is critical for engagement and long-term learning. Lastly, grades can cause stress and anxiety, which can negatively impact learning and well-being.

In contrast, feedback is considered to be a more engaging method of assessment. Feedback is process oriented, which means it helps students understand where they need to improve and how they can achieve their goals. It also encourages intrinsic motivation, fostering a genuine desire to learn and engage with the material. Furthermore, feedback can be personalized to address individual students' strengths and weaknesses and promote a sense of ownership over their learning.

In conclusion, grades may not be the most effective method of assessment to engage students in learning. Providing meaningful feedback that is timely, specific, balanced, and encourages dialogue can foster a deeper understanding and long-term retention of knowledge. Feedback also promotes intrinsic motivation and a genuine desire to learn, which can lead to more successful outcomes in the long run.

To shift from grading to feedback using Google Apps, there are multiple tools you can integrate to provide students with personalized, timely, and meaningful feedback.

Create self-assessment forms with Google Forms for students to reflect on their learning process and identify areas where they were successful or need improvement. This encourages metacognition and self-regulated learning.

To provide students with feedback, consider using Google Keep. Keep notes are similar to sticky notes, but they are digital and collaborative. Create and share personalized notes in Google Keep with students, highlighting their strengths, areas for improvement, and actionable steps for growth.

The purpose of using the Rethinking Grading strategy in this way is to expose students to the following concepts:

1. Feedback, when used, improves outcomes.
2. Learning focuses on the process over the product.
3. Feedback is the beginning of a conversation, not the end.

> **TEMPLATE**
> Create a new Google Keep note by using your browser to go to keep.new. Set learning goals with students in a note. Keep notes are shareable with the student, so both you and the student can check in on the learning goals.

39. Integrating Peer Feedback

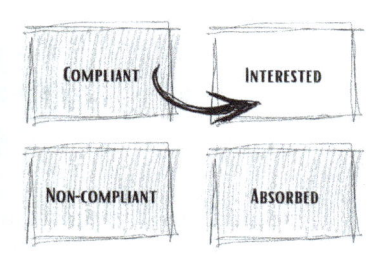

If, at the end of a test, you tell students, "Make sure you check your work," you are likely to see them compliantly flipping through the test and non-compliantly skimming over their work rather than actually checking their answers. Why? The students are spent. They used their fuel to answer the questions the first time, and they know what they meant to answer.

When you're already familiar with your own work and fatigued by the effort of creating it, it's easy to see how mistakes can be made and then missed. This is where the adage "I get by with a little help from my friends" comes in. Obviously, you are unlikely to ask students to exchange papers during a test and ask them to check someone else's work. However, peer reviewing is extremely powerful for formative work. Since students are unfamiliar with the work of their peers and less emotionally connected to others, work than their own, they are more likely to catch what the original author missed.

In fact, many people can become highly engaged in finding others' errors and/or helping others improve their work. Those who like to find others' errors are often fueled by a competitive nature. Those who prefer to help others improve are often fueled by kindness. Recognizing the motivation for peer reviewing can help create conditions that align to the task and foster higher levels of engagement.

As well, peer reviewing gives students a chance to see not only others' mistakes but also other students' successes. The thinking that is required in identifying both is profound and helps the reviewer improve their own work.

Classrooms that provide students the opportunities to engage in peer feedback reinforce the value of formative learning by giving students the opportunity to improve. Doing so helps students see that learning is indeed a process, which means they can better focus on the learning rather than on grades.

Make peer feedback an integrated part of your classroom through the collaboration features in Google Apps. Google Docs, Sheets, and Slides all allow for students to insert comments on peer documents. Include in the assignment rubric that the assignment should include peer feedback, and expect that students will make improvements to their work based on that feedback.

Google Classroom users have student work automatically added to Google Drive. Create a new assignment titled "Peer Feedback" and add student documents as attachments. Change the default from STUDENTS CAN VIEW FILE to STUDENTS CAN EDIT FILE. This allows students to add feedback comments to peer work.

Create a rubric template in Google Sheets. On the first sheet of the workbook, add a list of student names. Use the "TemplateTab" add-on to duplicate the rubric within the same spreadsheet for each student. Share the spreadsheet with edit access to allow students to evaluate peer work against the rubric.

The purpose of using the Integrating Peer Feedback strategy in this way is to expose students to the following concepts:

1. Collaboration fosters a sense of community and encourages students to be more engaged in the learning process.
2. Taking an active role in the evaluation process, promoting critical thinking, self-reflection, and a deeper understanding of the subject matter.
3. Essential communication skills, such as active listening, empathy, and articulating thoughts clearly and respectfully.

> **TEMPLATE**
>
> In this Google Sheets template, you can paste your class roster into the tab "Put Roster Here." In the tab "Put Rubric Here," you can paste the rubric. Run the "TemplateTab" add-on to create a copy of the rubric per student. Make a copy of this spreadsheet per student to allow the students to evaluate any student in the class.
>
> **tinyurl.com/engagementpeereval**

40. Sharing in the Stream

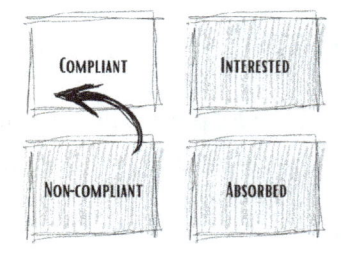

Belonging is an important aspect of relationship formation, so it is important for students to feel like they belong within a classroom. Since relationships are important to engagement, finding ways to create belonging leads to higher levels of engagement.

Online tools should not feel lonely or cold—they should be designed with a sense of community and belonging. Teachers need to find ways to explicitly build welcoming environments with high levels of rapport.

The Stream in Google Classroom is your classroom digital social space. Use the stream as a place for students to post information about what matters to them. Not only does this allow them to have some ownership of the space but it allows you to gain helpful insights into what students are interested in. Use this information to differentiate lesson activities and further build relationships. Help students feel that the Google Classroom is their shared space and not just the teacher's space.

Use the Stream to interact with students around prompts that help you to get to know them better. Post a question or prompt along with a display image to engage students in sharing their ideas or opinions.

> **TEMPLATE**
>
> Customize the Stream by creating a custom header image. Include images of students from class and change the banner image frequently to highlight more students. Encourage students to design the classroom header image.
>
> **tinyurl.com/engagementgcheader (Google Drawing Template)**
>
> Images make for a more engaging digital platform. Use these announcement image samples when creating posts to the Google Classroom Stream.
>
> **tinyurl.com/engagementannouncements**

The purpose of using the Sharing in the Stream strategy in this way is to expose students to the following concepts:

1. Shared ownership of the learning environment.
2. Building relationships and rapport.

It also allows teachers to:

1. Create additional spaces for students to socially interact.

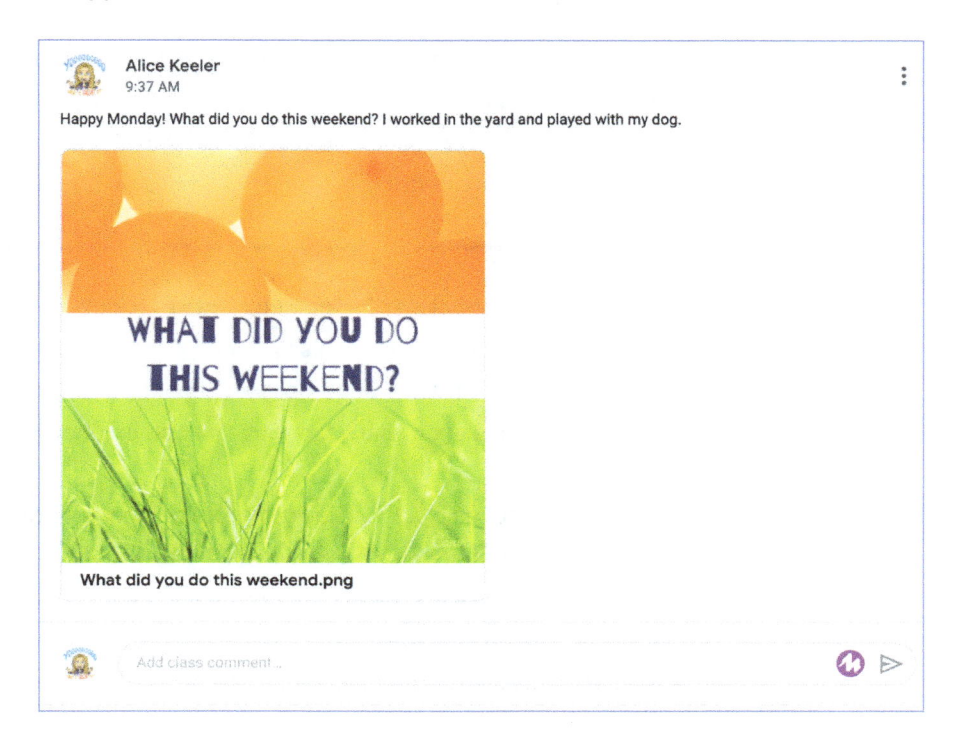

Alice Keeler
9:37 AM

Happy Monday! What did you do this weekend? I worked in the yard and played with my dog.

WHAT DID YOU DO THIS WEEKEND?

What did you do this weekend.png

Add class comment...

41. Tapping into Student Expertise

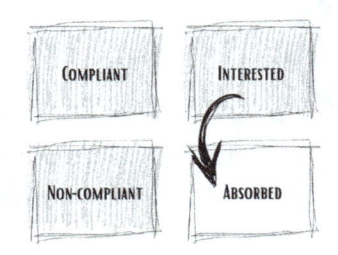

In today's world, students are exposed to an abundance of information and opportunities outside of the classroom. Extracurricular activities, hobbies, and personal interests can be incredibly engaging and rewarding for students, often more so than the required curriculum. However, this doesn't mean that the classroom should be overlooked as a prime location for learning. In fact, it is an essential part of a student's education, and by connecting what they're doing outside of school to the required content standards, we can create a more engaging and relevant learning experience.

Students are constantly learning new things, whether it's through participating in clubs or hobbies, pursuing personal interests, or engaging in community service. These activities may require skills and knowledge that are directly related to the content standards taught in the classroom. By connecting these experiences to the required curriculum, we can help students see the relevance and applicability of what they're learning.

Furthermore, by encouraging students to design their own learning experiences, we can tap into their natural curiosity and motivation to learn. This approach allows students to take ownership of their learning and pursue topics that are of genuine interest to them. By doing so, we can create a more personalized and engaging learning environment that fosters a love of learning and a deeper understanding of the content.

In other words, by connecting what students are doing outside of school to the required content standards, we can create a more engaging and relevant learning experience that taps into their natural curiosity and motivation to learn. This approach allows students to take ownership of their learning and develop a deeper understanding of the content while pursuing topics that are of genuine interest to them.

What are your students doing outside of class? Provide students a Google Form to fill out with descriptions of things they spend time on outside of school and also provide a dropdown list of the standards to choose from. Ask students to explain how what they accomplished connects to course objectives. Additionally, provide a question to provide evidence such as a descriptive narrative, photos, or links.

You can add your standards or objectives to a Google Form from a document or spreadsheet and copy them with Ctrl+C then paste the entire list at once into the Google Form with Ctrl+V. (Note that the list needs to have each item on a different line.) Add a question to the Form and change the question type to Dropdown. Pasting the entire list into the Option 1 spot will create a separate option for each option.

Since students will fill out the form infrequently, consider setting up an email notification from the Form when it is filled out. On the RESPONSES tab of the Google Form, use the three-dots menu to select GET EMAIL NOTIFICATIONS FOR NEW RESPONSES.

Determine how you will provide students with course credit for their demonstration of learning. One option is to offer credit in place of an existing assignment in the gradebook. Another approach is to create a new assignment and assign it only to the student who has demonstrated the learning. Alternatively, you could add some assignments to the gradebook that encourage student-directed learning and assign points based on their performance. In any case, it is important to make a comment in the gradebook to indicate which activity the student is receiving credit for.

The purpose of using the Tapping into Student Expertise strategy in this way is to expose students to the following concepts:

1. Learning is not confined to a classroom or even a school.

It also allows teachers to:

1. Find appropriate and engaging ways to connect the standards to their learning.
2. Use students' interests outside of school to get students interested in school.

> **TEMPLATE**
>
> This Google Form template provides a starter for designing your own Form to accept student demonstrations of learning.
>
> **alicekeeler.com/engagementchoiceform**

42. Showing Growth with Student Portfolios

Have you ever been told that you have gotten better at something but lacked that awareness yourself? This is because growth is often incremental, so it can be difficult to spot—especially for the person who is doing the growing. This explains why when you visit family with small children who you don't see regularly, you will inevitably comment, "Wow! The kids have gotten so big!" You see the growth in a way that the parents may not because the parents see the children daily. You, on the other hand, only see the kids occasionally, so your ability to see the growth is easier.

Student portfolios are a great way to provide a figurative measuring stick for students to see how much they have grown, since it's often easy to forget how little they knew when they started a class.

A portfolio is not a notebook of all student work. Instead, it highlights work that best shows progress. And best doesn't mean only the work that earned full credit; it means the work that does the best job showing what the student knew at the time. These "best" samples may be things they actually failed at, along with their reflections.

Reflections are an essential part of the learning process. A portfolio should give students an opportunity to explain what they learned. Sometimes what they learned is from their mistakes and not just their successes. The work alone doesn't fully demonstrate what students learned from the process; having students add text or videos to explain learning can be a more meaningful way to assess what students got out of an activity.

Students can use Google Sites or Google Slides for their portfolio. Either of these allow for students to add pictures of their work and text to explain their learning. What is important is that the elements are chosen by the student to tell a story of their learning.

Create a new Google Sites at sites.new. Design a template to help students to include the required elements of their portfolio, including reflections.

Go to sites.google.com and choose the TEMPLATE GALLERY to upload your student portfolio template by choosing it from Google Drive. Once it's added to the school domain, students will be able to locate the template to create a copy for themselves. Have students add you, the teacher, to their Google Site as an editor. This will allow you to find student work in your Google Drive.

> **TEMPLATE**
>
> This document is a guideline for teachers with tips to help them to create templates for portfolios.
>
> **tinyurl.com/Engagement-Portfolio**

Since Google Sites reside in Google Drive, students can add their portfolio to an assignment in Google Classroom. This will automatically add the teachers of the class to the student Google Sites portfolio. However, students will lose editing access upon submission. It is important to quickly return the assignment in Google Classroom to allow students to continue to work on their portfolios.

The purpose of using the Showing Growth with Student Portfolios strategy in this way is to expose students to the following concepts:

1. Growth is incremental and hard to see in real time.
2. They have the ability to monitor and reflect on their own growth.
3. Reflection is a key aspect of learning.

4. The best work does not have to be the work with the highest grades; it can be the work that creates the most reflection on learning.

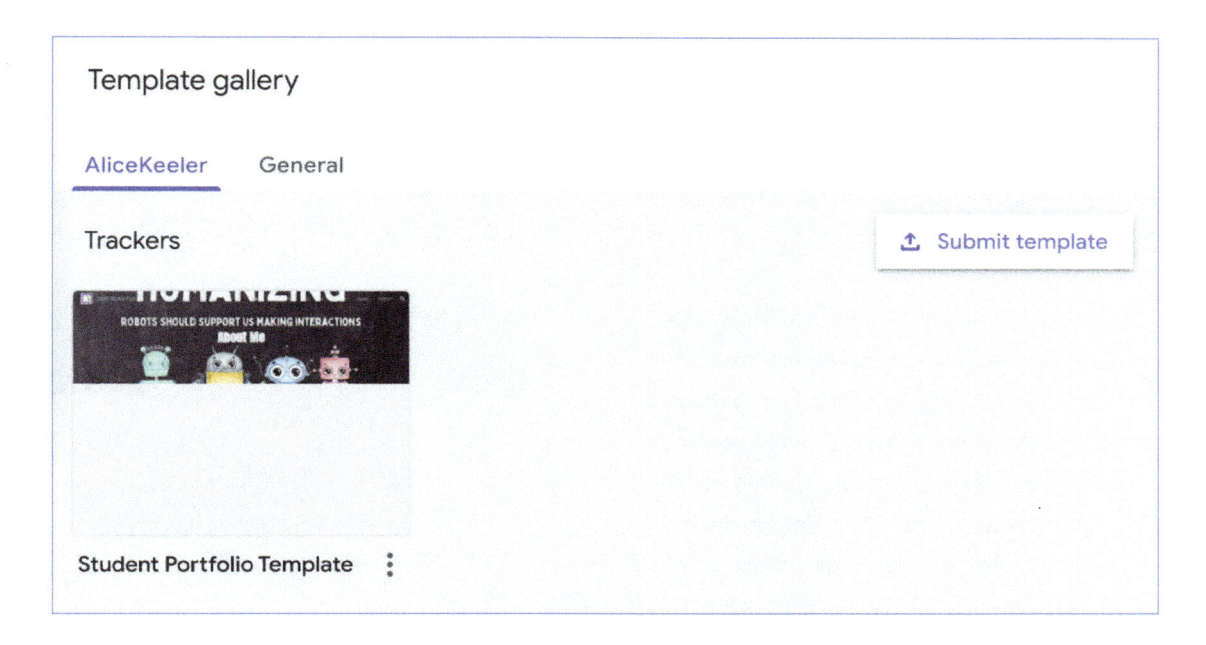

43. Embarking on Quest Chains

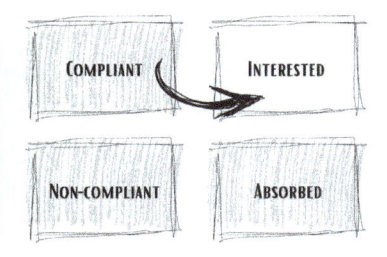

A task that is beyond a student's zone of proximal development can be overwhelming and cause a student to not even want to try. How many times have we worked with a student and said, "Okay, let's just break this down, what do we do first?" Instead of giving students the complete task at once, let's learn from the way video games scaffold a skill.

Video games are designed to work within one's zone of proximal development. The first level is often very easy so you can see the basics of what you will need to do. Then, the game really starts. There, you will almost certainly lose a few times before you progress to the next level.

Quest chains are tasks that all students will do—they just do not have to do them all at the same pace. This is similar to a video game where all players will complete the level—they get to be self-paced through the experience.

50 Ways to Engage Students with Google Apps

In a quest chain, completing a task unlocks the next one in the series. (This is different from a choice board, where students are given options regarding what they want to do.)

To create a quest chain system using a Google Sheets spreadsheet, you can use an If statement to hide each step until the previous one is completed.

To do this, design the spreadsheet with a list of tasks or instructions, but only reveal one at a time. Require students to add evidence or indicate completion in a designated column. If the previous cell is empty, the next step should remain empty. Using double quotes within the If statement allows the spreadsheet to check for a blank cell. If the cell is blank, the next step will also be blank. If the cell is not blank, the next step in the quest chain will be revealed.

To create the formula, start a cell with an equals sign and type If followed by a left parenthesis:

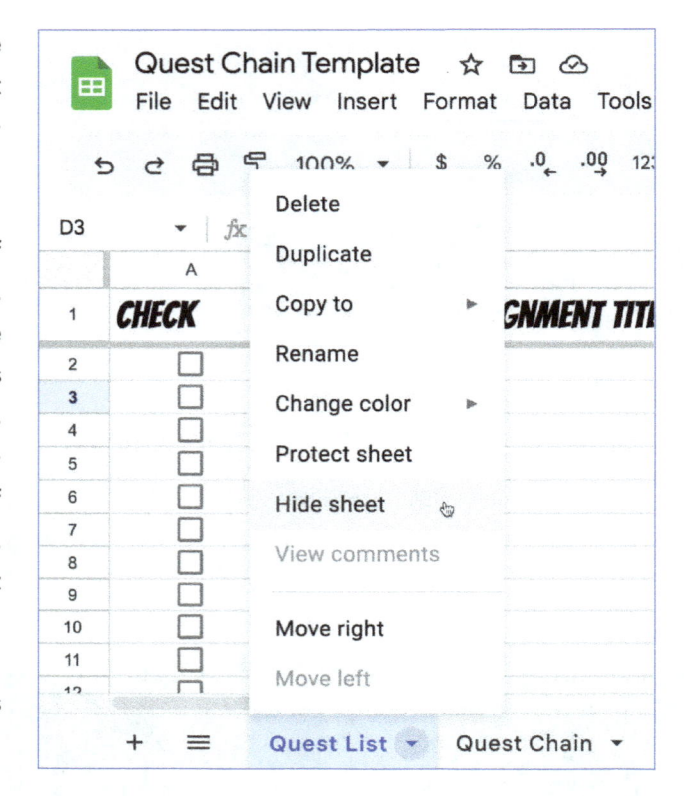

=if(

Then enter the cell range of the value that must be completed before showing the next question option. Use double quotation marks to indicate that the formula should check for a blank cell. Then, add a comma and another set of double quotations. The third element of the formula is the text that will be displayed to the student if the cell is not blank.

For example, the formula might look like this:

=If(C3= "", "", "Create a Google Doc.")

> **TEMPLATE**
>
> In this template, create a list of steps on the first tab, "Quest List." Click on the tiny triangle on the tab to HIDE SHEET. The remaining tab, "Quest Chain," will reveal the next step after the previous step is checked off.
>
> tinyurl.com/engagementquestchain

The purpose of using the Embarking on Quest Chains strategy in this way is to expose students to the following concepts:

1. Not every student needs to be at the same place in the learning as long as they achieve the learning.
2. Scaffolding learning is helpful no matter where you are in the learning journey.
3. Being at an appropriate pace fuels engagement.

44. Choosing Adventure

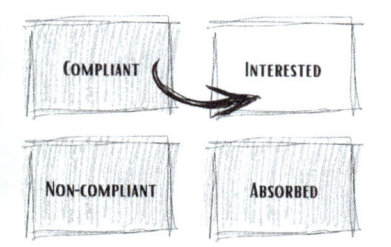

Remember how Tom Sawyer got out of painting Aunt Polly's fence? He tricked the other kids into believing painting was fun and that he didn't want to share this great experience with anyone. In reality, anyone who has painted a fence knows it's drudgery. Yet Tom Sawyer not only conned the other kids, he got them to pay him for the opportunity.

People often prefer doing a task when it's framed as a game instead of as a chore, because games can add an element of fun and excitement to an otherwise mundane activity. When a task is presented as a game, it can engage a person's natural sense of play and make the task feel more enjoyable and rewarding.

Games can also provide a clear set of rules and objectives, which can help people stay focused and motivated as they work toward a goal. In contrast, chores often lack clear guidelines and can feel overwhelming or monotonous, which can make it difficult for people to stay motivated.

When a task is presented as a game, there is a sense of accomplishment and progress as players work through different levels or challenges. This can provide a feeling of satisfaction and pride in one's achievements, which can be a powerful motivator.

Since games often have choices the players have to make, they can provide a sense of autonomy and control over the task at hand. Players can often choose how they approach a challenge or problem, which can make the task feel more personal and engaging. In contrast, chores are often assigned and may not allow for much flexibility or creativity.

Check out the games and experiences Google offers in Google Arts & Culture. For example, one of the games, *Where Is Hopper*, provides an AI adventure. Not only is this game—and others on the Arts & Culture site—educational, it shows us some ways that digital tools can engage learners.

After playing this adventure game on Google Arts & Culture, have students design their own adventure that incorporates a target standard for your class.

In Google Slides, students can use Ctrl+K to hyperlink pictures and text to other slides. The slides are designed to be nonlinear to allow the user to make choices and be taken to different parts in the adventure. Students can use the FILE menu in Google Slides to select PUBLISH TO THE WEB. This published link provides a view-only experience of their Google Slides that can be shared with peers. Have students interact with peers' adventure games to help them engage more with class content.

The purpose of using the Choosing Adventure strategy in this way is to expose students to the following concepts:

1. What success looks like (since games have different levels or progress markers).

It also allows teachers to:

1. Find ways to take mundane tasks and build interest.
2. Personalize tasks for students.

> **TEMPLATE**
>
> Use this Google Slides template to assign students to design their own game that allows the player to make choices. Students will want to add navigation buttons to the slides for player choices.
>
> **tinyurl.com/engagementadventureslides**

45. Discovering Google Arts & Culture

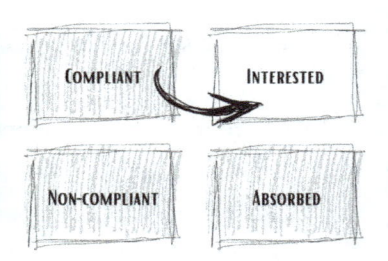

Just like books are important to all content areas—not just English classes—art is important to all content areas, not just art classes. Not only can art enhance creativity and imagination in your students, it encourages them to think creatively and to come up with original ideas. Art can also promote self-expression and communication in your students, allowing them to express themselves in a way that words cannot. This can be especially helpful for students who may struggle with verbal communication.

Art can also enrich cultural understanding and appreciation, teaching students about different cultures, customs, and traditions and helping them to appreciate and value the diversity of human experience and expression.

Finally, art can enhance learning in other subjects, making abstract concepts more concrete and easier to understand and serving as a source of inspiration and motivation for learning.

Google Arts & Culture (artsandculture.google.com) is a free website and app developed by Google that allows users to explore and discover art, artifacts, and cultural objects from around the world. This digital platform brings together millions of works of art and cultural objects from over two thousand museums, galleries, and institutions in over seventy countries.

Students can browse a variety of collections, including paintings, sculptures, photographs, drawings, prints, and more. The website also offers virtual tours of museums and cultural sites as well as interactive exhibits and educational resources. In addition, students can use the website's search function to find specific works of art or objects, or to discover new art and culture based on their interests.

Google Arts & Culture updates frequently with new educational games and interactive experiences. Regularly revisit the Arts & Culture website to consider what new offerings it provides that can create engaging experiences for your students.

Here are just a few ways you could use Google Arts & Culture:

- Use the virtual tours and interactive exhibits to supplement in-class discussions and lessons on art history and cultural studies.
- Use the collections and exhibits to inspire creative writing or art projects in the classroom.

TEMPLATE

Incorporating Google Arts & Culture can require creativity in seeing how what you are teaching relates to art. Ask Google Gemini to suggest a lesson plan in the 5 Es lesson plan model to create a lesson for the standard you are teaching and to integrate Google Arts & Culture. If the use of Google Arts & Culture that Google Gemini comes up with is a shallow integration, continue to prompt Gemini for more creative suggestions.

In the template we have generated several examples of AI lesson plans that use Google Arts & Culture. However, as should be the case with all AI use, we used critical analysis of the results and improved the lesson plans based on our experience of teaching students with technology.

tinyurl.com/engagementartlesson

- Use the resources to teach students about the role of art in social and political movements, and how it can be used to express ideas and opinions.
- Use the website to introduce students to different cultural traditions and customs from around the world.

The purpose of using the Discovering Google Arts & Culture strategy in this way is to expose students to the following concepts:

1. Art is a valuable part of the human experience.
2. The use of art isn't limited to art classes.
3. There are virtual resources that can enhance in-person learning.

46. Using Single-Point Rubrics

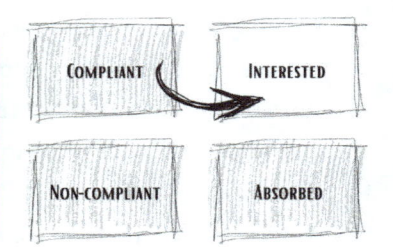

Most people are familiar with a standard rubric that has the criteria along the left-hand side and language in columns to the right of the criteria. In each cell, there is a description of what to expect at each level. If you're a teacher—particularly of a content area that is performance based like art, music, languages, and even physical education—you probably use rubrics regularly.

Despite the time teachers spend creating and using them, students are often overwhelmed and confused by the rubrics that are meant to provide them with the clarity they need to be successful with a task.

A single-point rubric is an innovative assessment tool that offers a simplified and focused approach to grading student work. It centers on a specific set of criteria or learning objectives, and rather than using multiple performance levels, it only describes the desired proficiency level. This simplicity can make it easier for students to understand the expectations and can increase student engagement since clarity and feedback lead to higher levels of investment and success.

A single-point rubric will typically list criteria in a middle column of a table and leave room on each side of the column for feedback.

Create a Google Sheets spreadsheet template with project requirements listed in Column B. Use Column A for "Concern areas that need work" and Column C for "Advanced evidence of exceeding standards."

Widen the column widths, and set wrap on the cells and both vertical and horizontal centering.

The purpose of using the Using Single-Point Rubrics strategy in this way is to expose students to the following concepts:

1. Clearly articulated expectations lead to a better ability to work toward meeting those expectations.
2. Working toward improvement and growth, rather than solely aiming for a particular grade.

It also allows teachers to:

1. Provide more straightforward feedback that can help students feel more engaged and motivated to refine their work.

> **TEMPLATE**
>
> Use the "TemplateTab" add-on to insert a single-point rubric template into Google Sheets. After filling in the single-point criteria, duplicate the template for each student on your roster in the same spreadsheet. Paste your class roster onto the first sheet in the spreadsheet, and use the EXTENSIONS menu to set up TemplateTab to paste your roster into the first sheet. In the advanced options for TemplateTab, set up SINGLE POINT ROSTER.
>
> List your criteria in column C. Run TemplateTab to allow you to easily provide feedback within the same spreadsheet. Optionally, export each completed rubric to its own spreadsheet to share with students.
>
> **alicekeeler.com/codedbyalice**

47. The Value of a Field Trip

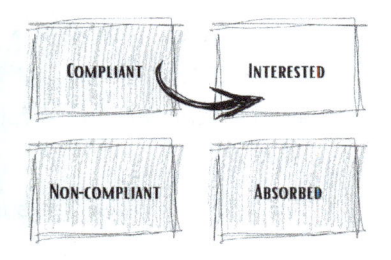

Students almost always love field trips, because the learning becomes experiential (not to mention the benefit of a change in their routines). Unfortunately, live field trips are expensive. From the price of admission to the location to the buses, field trips can be cost prohibitive. As well, there are many places that are impossible for people to visit directly—even more so when talking about younger students.

There are many premade virtual field trips (VFTs) that teachers can choose from, some free, some at a cost. Teachers can also create VFTs by curating different websites to personalize the experience for students based on the learning in a specific classroom.

In "Why Use Virtual Field Trips,"[3] Scott Mandel notes that the choice between using a packaged or a personalized field trip is similar to the choices made in the planning of a real-life excursion. For instance, if students go to a museum and are required to take a predetermined tour supplied by that museum, with no alterations or changes based on their classroom curriculum, that would be considered a real-life packaged field trip. However, if the teacher talks to the museum personnel and has the tour tailored to meet the specific curricular goals of the class, that is a personalized field trip.[4]

In short, there are times when a packaged VFT would be appropriate, just like a standard tour for a live field trip would be. Then there are times when you want something more customized.

While field trips that involve traveling to a location are amazing, we are limited by the places near us and the funds available.

Google Arts & Culture provides premade virtual field trips that not only save the cost of a bus but allow students to visit places too far to visit. Students can explore Mars, the bottom of the ocean, museums, and more!

Start by going to artsandculture.google.com/project/expeditions to find a virtual tour that ties in with units or topics that you are teaching.

The purpose of using the The Value of a Field Trip strategy in this way is to expose students to the following concepts:

1. Exploring settings and locations they cannot easily or ever visit in person.
2. Exploration leads to engagement.
3. Detours from the routine are stimulating for the brain.

> **TEMPLATE**
>
> An excellent way to start a lesson with the *engage* step from the 5 Es lesson plan model is to utilize a virtual field trip. In this example of a virtual trip to El Capitan, you provide students with a common shared experience that can be used to engage students in conversations around algebra functions.
>
> The field trip does not necessarily have to be directly related to the topic. For example, the virtual trip to El Capitan is not specifically a math lesson; however students have an opportunity to connect the functions lesson that follows the VFT back to the rock-climbing experience.
>
> **alicekeeler.com/elcap**

---

3   Scott Mandel, *Virtual Field Trips in the Cyberage: A Content Mapping Approach* (Chicago: Skylight Professional Development/Pearson, 1999).
4   Scott Mandel, "Why Use Virtual Field Trips?," http://www.phschool.com/eteach/professional_development/virtual_field_trips/essay.html."

48. Designing Collaborative Websites

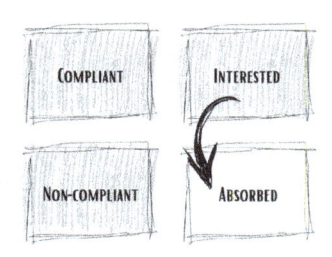

Before the internet, our worlds were smaller. Sharing ideas was often limited to only those people who you knew or knew you. Now, we have the opportunity to learn from people we have never met, and they have the opportunity to learn from us. We also have the ability to collaborate in real time to create and share.

Collaborative websites can be engaging for users because they involve a hands-on approach to learning and a creative outlet for self-expression. Users can experiment with different design elements, layouts, and colors to create a unique and visually appealing website that reflects their interests and style. Additionally, website creation provides a sense of ownership and pride as users see their ideas come to life in a tangible form.

Users can also benefit from the social interaction that comes with sharing their websites with others and receiving feedback, encouragement, and suggestions for improvement. The process of creating a website can be challenging, and for that very reason, it actually increases engagement. In this way, the challenge is a rewarding experience that stimulates the user's curiosity, problem-solving skills, and creativity.

Integrating collaborative tools such as Google Sites into your classroom can significantly enhance student engagement by fostering a sense of teamwork, promoting creativity, and encouraging active participation in the learning process.

Like a Google Doc, Google Sites can be shared and edited simultaneously by multiple people. And, like a Google Doc, Sites save to Google Drive. Have one student create a Google Site in Google Drive or simply start from sites.new. The SHARE icon in Sites is similar to Drive: it is the person icon in the toolbar. Each group member will need to be added as a collaborator on the Site.

One advantage to a Google Site over a Google Doc is multimedia. Students can embed Google Docs, Sheets, Slides, and videos directly into the Site. For more complex group projects, a Google Site is the ideal way to combine the different elements of the project.

Another advantage to Google Sites is that students can share their curated presentation of ideas with an outside audience. This may be others at the school, such as students, the librarian, or the principal. Additionally, when appropriate, the student work can be shared with parents and community members. Giving students an audience beyond the teacher can engage students by giving the project additional purpose.

It is important for students to realize that sharing permissions are not modified when embedding documents in Google Sites. A file in their Drive will always be visible to the student. However, the file embedded in Google Sites will not be visible to someone who is not a collaborator on the document. Help students to understand how to change file-sharing permissions to ANYONE CAN VIEW.

The purpose of using the Designing Collaborative Websites strategy in this way is to expose students to the following concepts:

1. Collective responsibility, which can motivate students to contribute their best efforts and remain engaged in the project.

> **TEMPLATE**
>
> Share this directions page digitally with students. This helps them to understand the steps to follow to share their group-collaboration site.
>
> **tinyurl.com/engagementgroupslides**

It also allows teachers to:

1. Enable students to work together simultaneously, which facilitates real-time communication, feedback, and problem-solving.
2. Expose students to a variety of ideas and viewpoints, which can lead to more innovative solutions and enhance critical thinking skills.
3. Provide students with the opportunity to be creative in the design and presentation of their work.

49. Coding

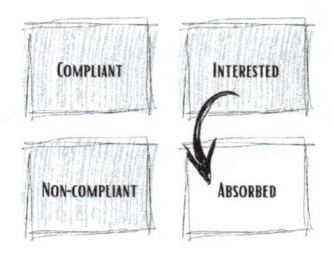

Learning to code can be an engaging and stimulating experience for students. Certainly, coding involves interactive and hands-on learning that encourages students to experiment and explore, both high-leverage ways to bolster engagement. After all, by applying the concepts they learn in class to real-world problems, students can see the immediate impact of their work, which can be both rewarding and motivating.

Additionally, coding provides opportunities for students to be creative and express their ideas through building websites, creating games, and designing apps. This can make learning more enjoyable and meaningful, as students feel a sense of ownership and pride in the projects they create.

Learning to code can also foster a sense of collaboration and community as students work together to solve problems and share ideas. This not only improves teamwork and communication skills but also enhances the learning experience by exposing students to different perspectives and approaches.

Finally, since coding is a skill that can be applied across many different fields and disciplines, from scientific research to the arts, it is something that students will find engaging no matter what their interests are. This makes coding a valuable asset for the classroom.

Google Apps Script allows students to create code (based on JavaScript) to modify Google Docs, Sheets, Slides, and Forms.

Students can access the script editor through the EXTENSIONS menu and then select APPS SCRIPT. Alternatively, they can go to script.google.com to create their code.

Encourage students to create games and projects with Google Apps by adding code to the Google App document to add functionality and interactivity to the project.

A simple code for students to get started with is to add a pop-up message to a Google Doc. In the Apps Script editor, add the following code:

```
function onOpen(){
DocumentApp.getUi()
.alert('Message goes here');
}
```

Students will need to ensure their message is enclosed in single quotations. Save and run the script to test the code. Exiting the Google Doc and reopening should automatically display the message.

> **TEMPLATE**
>
> The Getting Started with Google Apps Script: Essential JavaScript Knowledge can guide students to get started with using creative critical thinking to elevate what they can do with Google Workspace.
>
> **alicekeeler.com/engagementappsscript**

The purpose of using the Coding strategy in this way is to expose students to the following concepts:

1. A sense of community and teamwork, making the learning process more enjoyable and meaningful.

It also allows teachers to:

1. Use hands-on learning to encourage students to experiment and explore.

50. Collaborating via Email

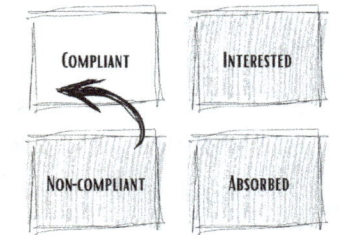

After getting a new cell phone, Heather thought everything was great. Then, someone told her they left her a voicemail message, but the phone didn't notify her of the message. Heather thought the person accidentally called the wrong phone. Then, it happened again with someone else. As it turned out, the phone was not providing Heather with voicemail notifications. Before customer service fixed the issue, Heather was panicked, worrying about what important information she may have missed.

In the twenty-first century, it's easy to forget the days before caller ID, voicemail, and email notifications were ubiquitous. These conveniences increase our ability to be in the know.

In school, we want the same for our students, since communication provides real-time feedback and direction even if the teacher and student are not physically in the same space. However, timing is everything. If students are not aware if or when the feedback is ready to view, they may either feel anxious and repeatedly look for it even if the teacher hasn't gotten to it yet, or they may forget to check because they have moved on to something else.

After giving students feedback in a Google Doc, Sheet, or Slides, use the FILE menu to select EMAIL. Use the option EMAIL COLLABORATORS.

The EMAIL COLLABORATORS option allows you to alert a student that you are ready for them to respond to the feedback that you left in the document. This feature automatically provides the student with the link back to the document, making it easy for them to quickly respond to the feedback.

Students can also use this feature to alert their teacher that they have made updates to the document based on feedback and are ready for assessment.

The purpose of using the Collaborating via Email strategy in this way is to expose students to the following concepts:

1. Sharing ideas, asking questions, and clarifying concepts.
2. Real-time collaboration provides timely guidance, feedback, and support.

It also allows teachers to:

1. Enhance digital literacy skills.

> **TEMPLATE**
>
> Make a copy of this template for students to complete their assignment in Google Docs. The template reminds the student to use the EMAIL COLLABORATORS feature to alert you that they are ready for feedback.
>
> **tinyurl.com/engagementemailcollab**

Conclusion

Student engagement is crucial for fostering an effective learning environment. True engagement is not about merely entertaining students or having fun, but creating challenging and rewarding learning experiences that inspire students to put in their best effort. When students are genuinely engaged, they work at the high end of their zone of proximal development, embracing challenges and failures as essential elements of the learning process.

To enhance student engagement, educators must be innovative and creative in their use of tools such as Google tools, ensuring they are used to facilitate learning in unique and empowering ways. By incorporating the 4 Cs (creative thinking, collaboration, communication, and critical thinking) into lessons and assignments, teachers can design learning experiences that better engage students.

Moreover, understanding the Depth of Knowledge framework and incorporating it into lesson design can help teachers create tasks with varying levels of mental complexity. Although higher DOK levels do not guarantee engagement, they provide opportunities for students to overcome challenges, which can increase their motivation and interest in learning.

The key to fostering true student engagement lies in striking a balance between challenge and reward, ensuring that learning experiences are not only aligned with learning outcomes but also cognitively stimulating and meaningful. By recognizing the importance of engagement and striving to create learning experiences that cater to students' diverse needs and interests, educators can inspire a passion for learning that leads to more impactful and lasting educational outcomes.

About the Authors

ABOUT ALICE KEELER

Alice Keeler is an esteemed authority in the intersection of educational technology and pedagogy, offering a multifaceted understanding that few in the field possess. A mother of five and an active math teacher, she brings practical experience and an authentic voice to the ever-evolving discourse on student engagement and educational best practices. Her Master's degree in Educational Media Design and Technology adds an academic layer to her hands-on insights, making her uniquely positioned to guide educators.

Alice's roles as a Google Certified Innovator, Google Developer Expert for Google Workspace, and Google Cloud Innovator Champion indicate not just familiarity but deep expertise in Google's suite of educational tools. However, Alice is keenly aware that the mere use of these tools is not a guarantee of student engagement. In her own words, "Paperless is not a pedagogy." Her focus is on the meaningful and effective integration of technology into the educational landscape, emphasizing that Google Apps are most powerful when used in conjunction with a nuanced understanding of what genuinely engages students.

With multiple books to her name, Alice is a prolific writer whose work serves as a practical guide for teachers and administrators alike. She offers actionable strategies backed by both technological acumen and classroom experience, focusing on how educators can go beyond the superficial use of technology to create truly engaging learning experiences.

Known for her exceptional skills with Google Sheets—earning her the title "Queen of Spreadsheets"—Alice's expertise is expansive, covering the entire Google Workspace suite. Her ability to leverage these tools for optimal classroom efficiency and student interaction is a testament to her qualification to speak to the subject of student engagement via technology.

As a global speaker and trainer, Alice brings her insights to an international audience, helping educators worldwide grasp the complexities of integrating technology in ways that are pedagogically sound. Her digital footprint also includes AliceKeeler.com, a comprehensive resource for educators, and a vibrant social media presence where she shares real-time insights into educational technology trends and best practices.

Alice Keeler's extensive classroom experience, robust academic background, and technical mastery make her an authoritative voice on how to elevate student engagement through strategic use of Google Apps. Her work is a vital resource for educators committed to adopting technology not just as a replacement for traditional tools, but as a means to enrich and transform the educational experience.

ABOUT HEATHER LYON

Heather Lyon has a PhD in Educational Administration and an EdM in Reading from the University at Buffalo. She is a consultant, speaker, blogger, and district administrator. Heather lives with her husband and three children, who make her smile and teach her the importance of patience and humor! In addition to this book, Heather has authored *Engagement Is Not a Unicorn (It's a Narwhal)* and *The BIG Book of Engagement Strategies*.

To contact Heather for speaking or consulting, please visit Heather's website, LyonsLetters.com, where you can also subscribe to her weekly blog posts. Please follow Heather on X at @LyonsLetters or on LinkedIn.

Acknowledgments

HEATHER LYON

I want to thank Alice Keeler. I'll never forget our first time talking. Your enthusiasm was obvious and contagious. I am still humbled by your respect and interest in my work. You are 100 percent true to your values and to students. I love that about you! Thank you for your collaboration and friendship.

I would have never met Alice Keeler if not for Melody McAllister. Thank you for setting the wheels into motion.

I would not have met Melody without EduMatch. Though EduMatch didn't publish this book, the work EduMatch does paved the path for me as an author. I will always be grateful to EduMatch's fearless trailblazer, Dr. Sarah Thomas, who took a chance on me.

Thank you to the team at DBC. You welcomed me with open arms, and I have felt truly respected throughout this process. I am thrilled to a part of the family!

I would like to extend my deepest gratitude to the readers who have journeyed with me through the pages of my previous books and my blog, LyonsLetters.com. Your unwavering support and encouragement have been a constant source of inspiration for my writing.

While I am a fairly confident person, my loved ones have always had even more confidence in me than I have in myself—especially Mom, Dad, Uncle Elliott, and Aunt Nancy. Thank you.

To Nolan, Lilia, and Oliver—you are my family bubble. To my person, Melissa—1 million avocados. To my brother, sam—You're the best funcle ever. To Emily—XOXO.

Finally, there is not a word for the unconditional love and gratitude I feel for and from my husband, Howard. You are my biggest fan. To say that I couldn't have done this without your support is not an exaggeration. Howard, I hope you see that the "brushstrokes in the corner" are yours. I love you.

More from Dave Burgess Consulting, Inc.

Since 2012, DBCI has published books that inspire and equip educators to be their best. For more information on our titles or to purchase bulk orders for your school, district, or book study, visit **DaveBurgessConsulting.com/DBCIbooks**.

MORE FROM THE *LIKE A PIRATE*™ SERIES

Teach Like a PIRATE by Dave Burgess
eXPlore Like a PIRATE by Michael Matera
Learn Like a PIRATE by Paul Solarz
Plan Like a PIRATE by Dawn M. Harris
Play Like a PIRATE by Quinn Rollins
Run Like a PIRATE by Adam Welcome
Tech Like a PIRATE by Matt Miller

LEAD LIKE A PIRATE™ SERIES

Lead Like a PIRATE by Shelley Burgess and Beth Houf
Balance Like a PIRATE by Jessica Cabeen, Jessica Johnson, and Sarah Johnson
Lead beyond Your Title by Nili Bartley
Lead with Appreciation by Amber Teamann and Melinda Miller
Lead with Collaboration by Allyson Apsey and Jessica Gomez
Lead with Culture by Jay Billy
Lead with Instructional Rounds by Vicki Wilson
Lead with Literacy by Mandy Ellis
She Leads by Dr. Rachael George and Majalise W. Tolan

LEADERSHIP & SCHOOL CULTURE

Beyond the Surface of Restorative Practices by Marisol Rerucha
Change the Narrative by Henry J. Turner and Kathy Lopes
Choosing to See by Pamela Seda and Kyndall Brown
Culturize by Jimmy Casas
Discipline Win by Andy Jacks

Escaping the School Leader's Dunk Tank by Rebecca Coda and Rick Jetter
Fight Song by Kim Bearden
From Teacher to Leader by Starr Sackstein
If the Dance Floor Is Empty, Change the Song by Joe Clark
The Innovator's Mindset by George Couros
It's OK to Say "They" by Christy Whittlesey
Kids Deserve It! by Todd Nesloney and Adam Welcome
Leading the Whole Teacher by Allyson Apsey
Let Them Speak by Rebecca Coda and Rick Jetter
The Limitless School by Abe Hege and Adam Dovico
Live Your Excellence by Jimmy Casas
Next-Level Teaching by Jonathan Alsheimer
The Pepper Effect by Sean Gaillard
Principaled by Kate Barker, Kourtney Ferrua, and Rachael George
The Principled Principal by Jeffrey Zoul and Anthony McConnell
Relentless by Hamish Brewer
The Secret Solution by Todd Whitaker, Sam Miller, and Ryan Donlan
Start. Right. Now. by Todd Whitaker, Jeffrey Zoul, and Jimmy Casas
Stop. Right. Now. by Jimmy Casas and Jeffrey Zoul
Teachers Deserve It by Rae Hughart and Adam Welcome
Teach Your Class Off by CJ Reynolds
They Call Me "Mr. De" by Frank DeAngelis
Thrive through the Five by Jill M. Siler
Unmapped Potential by Julie Hasson and Missy Lennard
When Kids Lead by Todd Nesloney and Adam Dovico
Word Shift by Joy Kirr
Your School Rocks by Ryan McLane and Eric Lowe

TECHNOLOGY & TOOLS

50 Things to Go Further with Google Classroom by Alice Keeler and Libbi Miller
50 Things You Can Do with Google Classroom by Alice Keeler and Libbi Miller
140 Twitter Tips for Educators by Brad Currie, Billy Krakower, and Scott Rocco
Block Breaker by Brian Aspinall
Building Blocks for Tiny Techies by Jamila "Mia" Leonard
Code Breaker by Brian Aspinall
The Complete EdTech Coach by Katherine Goyette and Adam Juarez
Control Alt Achieve by Eric Curts
The Esports Education Playbook by Chris Aviles, Steve Isaacs, Christine Lion-Bailey, and Jesse Lubinsky
Google Apps for Littles by Christine Pinto and Alice Keeler
Master the Media by Julie Smith
Raising Digital Leaders by Jennifer Casa-Todd
Reality Bytes by Christine Lion-Bailey, Jesse Lubinsky, and Micah Shippee, PhD
Sail the 7 Cs with Microsoft Education by Becky Keene and Kathi Kersznowski
Shake Up Learning by Kasey Bell
Social LEADia by Jennifer Casa-Todd
Stepping Up to Google Classroom by Alice Keeler and Kimberly Mattina
Teaching Math with Google Apps by Alice Keeler and Diana Herrington
Teachingland by Amanda Fox and Mary Ellen Weeks
Teaching with Google Jamboard by Alice Keeler and Kimberly Mattina

TEACHING METHODS & MATERIALS

All 4s and 5s by Andrew Sharos
Boredom Busters by Katie Powell
The Classroom Chef by John Stevens and Matt Vaudrey
The Collaborative Classroom by Trevor Muir
Copyrighteous by Diana Gill
CREATE by Bethany J. Petty
Deploying EduProtocols by Kim Voge, with Jon Corippo and Marlena Hebern
Ditch That Homework by Matt Miller and Alice Keeler
Ditch That Textbook by Matt Miller
Don't Ditch That Tech by Matt Miller, Nate Ridgway, and Angelia Ridgway
EDrenaline Rush by John Meehan
Educated by Design by Michael Cohen, The Tech Rabbi
The EduProtocol Field Guide by Marlena Hebern and Jon Corippo
The EduProtocol Field Guide: Book 2 by Marlena Hebern and Jon Corippo
The EduProtocol Field Guide: Math Edition by Lisa Nowakowski and Jeremiah Ruesch
The EduProtocol Field Guide: Social Studies Edition by Dr. Scott M. Petri and Adam Moler
Empowered to Choose by Andrew Easton
Expedition Science by Becky Schnekser
Frustration Busters by Katie Powell
Fully Engaged by Michael Matera and John Meehan
Game On? Brain On! by Lindsay Portnoy, PhD
Guided Math AMPED by Reagan Tunstall
Innovating Play by Jessica LaBar-Twomy and Christine Pinto
Instructional Coaching Connection by Nathan Lang-Raad
Instant Relevance by Denis Sheeran
Keeping the Wonder by Jenna Copper, Ashley Bible, Abby Gross, and Staci Lamb
LAUNCH by John Spencer and A.J. Juliani
Learning in the Zone by Dr. Sonny Magana
Lights, Cameras, TEACH! by Kevin J. Butler
Make Learning MAGICAL by Tisha Richmond
Pass the Baton by Kathryn Finch and Theresa Hoover
Project-Based Learning Anywhere by Lori Elliott
Pure Genius by Don Wettrick
The Revolution by Darren Ellwein and Derek McCoy
The Science Box by Kim Adsit and Adam Peterson
Shift This! by Joy Kirr
Skyrocket Your Teacher Coaching by Michael Cary Sonbert
Spark Learning by Ramsey Musallam
Sparks in the Dark by Travis Crowder and Todd Nesloney
Table Talk Math by John Stevens
Unpack Your Impact by Naomi O'Brien and LaNesha Tabb
The Wild Card by Hope and Wade King
Writefully Empowered by Jacob Chastain
The Writing on the Classroom Wall by Steve Wyborney
You Are Poetry by Mike Johnston
You'll Never Guess What I'm Thinking About by Naomi O'Brien
You'll Never Guess What I'm Saying by Naomi O'Brien

INSPIRATION, PROFESSIONAL GROWTH & PERSONAL DEVELOPMENT

Be REAL by Tara Martin
Be the One for Kids by Ryan Sheehy
The Coach ADVenture by Amy Illingworth
Creatively Productive by Lisa Johnson
Educational Eye Exam by Alicia Ray
The EduNinja Mindset by Jennifer Burdis
Empower Our Girls by Lynmara Colón and Adam Welcome
Finding Lifelines by Andrew Grieve and Andrew Sharos
The Four O'Clock Faculty by Rich Czyz
How Much Water Do We Have? by Pete and Kris Nunweiler
PheMOMenal Teacher by Annick Rauch
P Is for Pirate by Dave and Shelley Burgess
A Passion for Kindness by Tamara Letter
The Path to Serendipity by Allyson Apsey
Recipes for Resilience by Robert A. Martinez
Rogue Leader by Rich Czyz
Sanctuaries by Dan Tricarico
Saving Sycamore by Molly B. Hudgens
The Secret Sauce by Rich Czyz
Shattering the Perfect Teacher Myth by Aaron Hogan
Stories from Webb by Todd Nesloney
Talk to Me by Kim Bearden
Teach Better by Chad Ostrowski, Tiffany Ott, Rae Hughart, and Jeff Gargas
Teach Me, Teacher by Jacob Chastain
Teach, Play, Learn! by Adam Peterson
The Teachers of Oz by Herbie Raad and Nathan Lang-Raad
TeamMakers by Laura Robb and Evan Robb
Through the Lens of Serendipity by Allyson Apsey
Write Here and Now by Dan Tricarico
The Zen Teacher by Dan Tricarico

CHILDREN'S BOOKS

The Adventures of Little Mickey by Mickey Smith Jr.
Alpert by LaNesha Tabb
Alpert & Friends by LaNesha Tabb
Beyond Us by Aaron Polansky
Cannonball In by Tara Martin
Dolphins in Trees by Aaron Polansky
I Can Achieve Anything by MoNique Waters
I Want to Be a Lot by Ashley Savage
The Magic of Wonder by Jenna Copper, Ashley Bible, Abby Gross, and Staci Lamb
Micah's Big Question by Naomi O'Brien
The Princes of Serendip by Allyson Apsey
Ride with Emilio by Richard Nares
A Teacher's Top Secret Confidential by LaNesha Tabb
A Teacher's Top Secret: Mission Accomplished by LaNesha Tabb
The Wild Card Kids by Hope and Wade King
Zom-Be a Design Thinker by Amanda Fox